FOREWORD BY DR. CHERE M. GOODE

I AM A VICTOR

Presented by

Dr. Cheryl Wood

ISBN: 978-1-7923-6383-2
Kindle ISBN: 978-1-7923-6384-9

TABLE OF CONTENTS

I AM A VICTOR!

FOREWORD
BY DR. CHERE M. GOODE

I recently experienced one of the most devastating losses imaginable to a mother. The loss of my 20-year-old son Jordan Alexander Cofield in a tragic motorcycle accident rocked me to my core. It honestly felt like someone punched me in the gut without warning and knocked the wind out of me and there was nothing I could do about it. I cried, screamed, questioned if it was real, and at times I even questioned my own sanity. Some days I couldn't even force myself to get out of bed. The thought of moving forward with life without my baby boy Jordan was unimaginable.

In life there are things that happen to us that can make us feel defeated, hopeless, and even insane but you can come out victorious with determination, will power, and prayer. What I love about this book is not only the raw, transparent stories of defeat and trials that challenged the authors but the hope it gives to so many others who may go through similar trials, trauma, and hurt. This book teaches that quitting is not an option. We must rise up each day and heal from whatever it was that hurt us. Not allowing what hurt us to haunt us. There truly is light at the end of every dark tunnel.

Regardless of how grim things may appear you can be victorious. Some ways to begin your journey of becoming a victor includes acknowledging the hurt and what caused it, allowing yourself to feel whatever and however you feel, accepting that it's okay to not be okay for as long as it takes to heal, reaching out for help from others who have experienced similar trauma or pain, taking things day by day to heal, and giving yourself grace and mercy to recover.

I AM A VICTOR!

This book will truly encourage, inspire, and motivate others to be resilient and heal. To be a victor. I AM A VICTOR!

Dr. Chere M. Goode
Recharge Strategist
www.totalharmonyenterprises.com

INTRODUCTION
BY DR. CHERYL WOOD

Visionary of *I Am A Victor*
13x Best-Selling Author | International Empowerment Speaker |
TEDx Speaker | Speaker Development Coach | Leadership Expert

There is no human being whose life has only been a bed of roses. Every human has faced challenges, obstacles, setbacks and roadblocks on their life journey. Despite the fact that all of us get knocked down, not all of us stay down. There are individuals, like each co-author in this book, who make a choice to get back up and keep fighting. There are individuals who commit to doing whatever it takes to emerge as a VICTOR instead of a VICTIM to their circumstances and the 'blows' that life throws their way.

I Am A Victor is a powerful compilation of the authentic stories of men and women who chose to get back up. In this book, you will get an exclusive opportunity to "hear" the personal and powerful testimonies about their commitment to claiming victory over some of life's most challenging obstacles. *I Am A Victor* will pull at your heartstrings and inspire you to claim your own personal power over every challenge you might face in order to become the greatest version of yourself. This powerful collection of stories demonstrates the bold, tenacious, and resilient spirit of men and women globally who refuse to throw in the towel even when the going gets tough.

I celebrate each of the co-authors of the *I Am A Victor* project for boldly sharing their truth – the good, the bad, the ugly, the uncertain, the setbacks and the victory. Each story will unveil the co-author's unique struggles and how they shifted their mindset, their attitude, and

9

their actions in order to overcome their challenges and, ultimately, find victory. As you immerse yourself in the *I Am A Victor* book, you will be reminded that no struggle can hold you back from fulfilling your destiny unless you allow it to. The stories will reignite a fire inside of you to persevere through everything that is meant to break you because there is always something greater on the other side of the pain. After all, a diamond is only created under extreme and intense pressure!

In my own personal life, I had to go on a journey of discovering that I could choose to be a victor over anything life threw my way. As a young girl who was raised in poverty in an inner-city housing project in Baltimore, Maryland, I assumed that my life would be dictated by my environment. I assumed that I would just be another statistic like the other youth in my neighborhood because that's the thinking that was instilled in me in that environment. Despite that toxic thinking, there was a turning point when I started to think for myself. I made a decision that I didn't want to be another statistic, I didn't want to be a victim. Instead, I wanted to be a VICTOR! So, I started to back my decision to do more and become more with consistent actions which led to my victory over my past and my circumstances.

Today, I thank God that I equipped myself with the tools to soar beyond all toxic thinking, obstacles, roadblocks, and challenges that threatened to hold me hostage to a life of lack instead of a life of abundance. I thank God that I had stories to read of other people who had claimed victory over their circumstances so that I could be inspired to forge my own path to success and creating the reality that I desired. And, as a result of my own victory, I accepted the responsibility to share my story of how God brought me through some of life's most difficult challenges including trauma and loss, in order to help others. As I bounced back from every challenge, I became more aware and confident about who I am and whose I am, and more conscious of the need to share my experiences. And every co-author in this book has the same mindset which is why they are courageously and vulnerably sharing their stories and their truth to inspire you.

Every time an individual shares their story, not only do they create freedom for themselves, but they also create hope for other individuals who are inspired to endure. That is what makes our lives matter... being willing to share our unique experiences, knowledge, lessons learned, and even the unforeseen, sometimes messy, parts of our lives so that someone else is inspired enough to persevere through their own struggle, learn their own lessons, overcome their own trauma, triumph over their own setbacks, and/or develop more hope and belief in their own dreams.

As you take a deep dive into *I Am A Victor*, you will see that each story is unique in its own right and that each co-author faced their own set of challenges, discouragement, grief, courage, hope, belief, and victory. Ultimately, you will see that no matter how successful or accomplished an individual is, they do not arrive there without fighting to overcome struggles.

It is my hope that you will read this book and feel more equipped, empowered, and inspired than ever before to keep pressing through your own journey without giving up, and to reach back and share your story so that you too can inspire others. And, most importantly, to remember that just as each of the co-authors is a VICTOR BY CHOICE, that you can be too!

Dr. Cheryl Wood
Visionary of *I Am A Victor*
WEBSITE: www.cherylempowers.com
EMAIL: info@cherylwoodempowers.com
SOCIAL MEDIA: @CherylEmpowers

I AM A VICTOR!

VANESSA K. ANTRUM

Surviving The Scars With A Smile
By Vanessa K. Antrum

It all began when I graduated from the 11th grade. It was the fall of 1976, and I was excited to be the youngest member of the freshman class at Allegheny College. But something wasn't right. My left breast was hurting so bad. She immediately bought me a ticket to fly home so that I could go to the doctor. I was 17 years old. My doctor discovered the first lump I ever had during that appointment, and I was scheduled for a biopsy. Back in the day, the biopsy procedure was very invasive. I endured all that – a scared little teenager - only to find out that it was a benign cyst. Little did I know, that would be the beginning of my journey with breast issues.

After that, I experienced numerous biopsies on my breasts because doctors always wanted to make sure that there wasn't something else going on. I became numb to repeatedly going through this process. In December 2004, I went to have my annual mammogram and was waiting for the results. I became really sick and took any over-the-counter medications I could. I was only masking the real sickness. The pain became worse, and I didn't know if it was a cold or the flu – but I knew I felt horrible. I went to the hospital and had emergency surgery for appendicitis.

In mid-January, I had recuperated from the appendectomy and was called in for the mammogram results. Because I was used to this routine, I didn't expect any bad news, but I was about to join a club that I never wanted to be a part of. What was about to happen would change my life forever. I went into the doctor's office. She had two

14

bottles of water and a box of tissues in front of her, waiting to explain everything. She told me everything that was going on, but the words, "Mrs. Antrum – we've found cancer," was what I remembered most. It was decided that I would have a mastectomy. After that, all I heard was The Charlie Brown teacher's voice "wah wah wah." And then something clicked - it was her voice saying – "Vanessa, listen to me, we're going to get through this. You're going to be alright."

I left and met my husband, Thomas, and talked and talked. Immediately, I found comfort in him. He was going to be there for me no matter what (and he still is). We prayed, and I found comfort in Jesus. We were going to fight this and were going to fight it together! I was so scared, but I knew I had to be strong. Receiving a diagnosis like this was hard. Did I have the faith to get through this? I thought so, but I tell you, I questioned that over and over again! I had to wait from January to April 15 to get the cancerous tumor out of my body.

It was such a weird feeling that something was growing inside me, and there was nothing I could do about it. How was I supposed to act? I wanted to cry every time I thought about it. Am I going to die? Will I see my children walk down the aisle? Will I be a grandma? Did I do something to deserve this? (That was really hard to shake). Why was this happening to me? Breast cancer doesn't run in my family, so I thought. Why is this happening to me, Lord? It wasn't immediate – trust me, it took a while – but the Lord answered my prayers, saying, "You are healed, and there will be no scars." Now that really blew my mind! Not only because I was going to be healed but because I suffered from keloid scars in the past, I was excited that I wouldn't have any scars. A few weeks later, I was praying with one of my friend's prayer partner. At the end of her prayer, she said, "God said, 'No more scars.'" I met with the plastic surgeon who would be doing the reconstruction surgery, and I told him about my concerns with keloids. He said, "Don't worry, there'll be no scars." What!!??!! That was confirmation! That thing rang in my ears so loud because that was what God had told me "No more scars." My husband and I told our

15

children, and the Lord led me to pray with them every day up until my surgery. We talked about death because it was real. We talked about life because it was real. And, we had to talk about cancer because that was what was in front of us at the time.

Have you ever expected things to go a certain way, and it didn't? Well, that's what happened to me. As people say, "It went left!" What happened? Had God given up on me? God said I was healed, but I was repeatedly going back and forth to the hospital. After my surgery, I was readmitted to the hospital five times! An infection had set in, and all of my incisions opened. I was so discouraged and in so much pain. Because I had recently had the appendectomy surgery, I was put on a wound vac machine to allow the incisions to heal without stitches as my body had not healed. Yeah, it was weird, but God allows people to invent things that heal people. But how do I claim victory in what seemed to be defeat? There I was - questioning God again. God, I thought you said, "No scars," but that's what I see. I SEE SCARS!!!

God did not leave me. In fact, He was there the whole time, and He had assigned angels to be there on my behalf. I distinctly remember three times I experienced angels while trying to heal. My family room became my hospital room. I had a hospital bed and other medical equipment there. One night I woke up with a dampness on my left side; something was oozing out of me. I did not want to go back to the hospital AGAIN, so we called the home nurse, who came immediately. The infection that was in my body had made a little pinhole and was coming out. I had a fever and was in a lot of pain. When the nurse arrived at my home, I could see a little "Daily Word' booklet in her pocket. I knew God was with me.

I was able to continue to recuperate at home. My family and friends were AWESOME! They learned how to give me my medicines through an IV and to change my surgical bandages. Thomas and my three daughters would get me set up for the day and then go to work/school. My parents would come after my family left, and they also provided care. Through all that I was experiencing, God allowed me to continue to smile and let my light shine. I made it through this journey to encourage women in my life.

I asked God to allow me to help others dealing with breast cancer. He opened so many doors for me: visiting women on their first night after they had a mastectomy at Doctor's Hospital, a radio interview, TV appearances, speaking at churches, serving on advisory groups, and working as a Breast Health Navigator for the Susan B Komen Foundation. I participated in a Survivor's pageant and was named the first runner up. I was inspired to do a mime to "Still I Rise" by Yolanda Adams for my talent. Since that time, I have shared this mime at churches, breast cancer events, and for people like the late Dr. Dorothy Height and Bishop Noel Jones.

You may be wondering about my physical scars that I mentioned earlier in my story. Yes, I have physical scars, but God was very intentional with his message about my scars. I was so focused on my physical scars, but God was gracious to help me with the emotional weight that turns to scars that can crush one going through breast cancer and literally take on a life force of its own. God did not let that become a reality in my life. My exuberant spirit and smile come from a deep, grateful place within that lets me know that God was with me, and He continues to shine brightly through me. So much so that when my family and I appeared as contestants on Family Feud, Steve Harvey told me, "Your high beams are on." I don't look back or feel any defeat. It had to happen for my growth and maturity. I AM HEALED, AND I HAVE NO SCARS!

As a reminder, please be sure to check your breasts. Get your yearly mammogram. Advocate for yourself. Trust God. Get support. I give all glory and honor to my Lord and Savior, Jesus Christ. He is the ultimate doctor, and He is still working miracles. I AM A VICTOR!

I AM A VICTOR!

BIO

Vanessa K. Antrum has been acknowledged as a light that shines to display God's goodness and mercy. Steve Harvey said when he met her "You got your high beams on." She is blessed to have survived both breast and kidney cancer and believes it is a testament to God's miraculous healing. An awesome trainer and motivational speaker, Vanessa loves encouraging others including her 4 adult children and 4 granddaughters. She has become a champion of self-care and caring for others by advocating for her elderly parents and still taking time to care for herself by giving herself the oxygen first. Vanessa has been interviewed on several TV shows to discuss her victories and share her voice of victory. She enjoys being married to her soul-mate, Thomas for 37 years.

Vanessa graduated from Allegheny College (Bachelors in Sociology/Speech Communications) and Howard University (Master of Social Work). Visit her online at www.vanessakantrum.com.

SUSAN APPLETON

THE EVOLUTION OF A FAT & BLACK GIRL
BY SUSAN APPLETON

Fat Black was my nickname, spoken as a term of love and endearment from my daddy to me. He would say, "Fat Black, if you give me a kiss, I'll give you one back." When he called me Fat Black, it was his way of uniquely connecting with me. My name meant nothing but love, and I didn't think of it any other way until I began to transition from elementary to middle school. It was then that how I saw myself began to shift. Despite being a well-rounded child, my beloved nickname began to take on a negative meaning for me. When I looked in the mirror, I saw a girl who was literally fat and black. You know, the girl with the "cute" face. I didn't know at the time, but this negative reflection of myself would follow me for a long time. It would impact my relationships, self-confidence, and how I perceived myself when I looked at others. It led me to make poor choices, experience unnecessary heartache, and stifled my growth.

Years later, I decided that I was going to be who God called me to be. I embraced the fact that I am black and beautiful. I am unique, worthy, and gifted. My journey of inner work began. I committed to facing my negative self-perceptions and shifted to loving myself unapologetically and completely. I began the Evolution of Fat Black.

HIDING IN PLAIN SIGHT
When my negative self-perception started, what I wanted most was to fit in and be accepted. I hated that my skin color or weight was often how I was described. I didn't know it then, but low self-esteem and lack of confidence had already begun, but how could that be? I lived in

20

the suburbs, in a two-parent household. I wasn't being abused and had older siblings who were doing well on their own. I was growing up in an environment built for success. Absolutely, but when you see yourself as less than, it makes you think differently. It's easy for the negative to overshadow the positive, and I didn't know how to talk about my feelings. I didn't know anyone else who had the same feelings as I did, and we didn't talk about things like that in my house. In my eyes, my siblings didn't have my issues. They were slim and bad to the bone. Because this was happening at the young age of twelve, talking to my mom didn't dawn on me. Sadly, I couldn't talk to my dad. I was silently angry at seeing him deal with his alcohol addiction. If he couldn't help himself, how was he going to help me?

I learned to keep my true feelings hidden. On the outside, I was outgoing and happy. I was loved, had two great best friends, and wonderful times with family. On the inside, I was angry and so unsure of myself. By the time I was in middle school, I had learned a few things about masking my insecurities. I discovered that I was smart and articulate, and if I focused on making good grades, I could stand out to my peers while hiding my feelings in plain sight. My family saw the academic scholar. My teachers saw a smart student who was a natural leader. However, my peers who I wanted to fit in with and be accepted by didn't make any moves to embrace me. So, I learned to master the art of false confidence. I spoke well and created an air about myself of being in control. Before I let anyone see me cry or share or my feelings, I would get silent, put on my confident face, and keep it moving. I practiced being confident to perfection, while inwardly hiding my feelings made me angry and hard. I used to say, "You could drop a brick from the sky, hit my shoulder, and I'd ask you what else you had," to describe how good I had become at hiding my insecurities.

THE EVOLUTION BEGINS
At sixteen, I started my first job. My boss, turned mentor, enforced a daily habit for me to see myself as beautiful, black, smart, and a well-

built young lady. She and my sister, who was eight years older than me, began to see what I was hiding. They pushed me to work on changing myself. It would take years to stop consenting to the negative thoughts of myself, but we have to start somewhere. They both saw my value and leadership potential battling against my low self-esteem, hurt, anger, and lack of confidence. My boss helped me peel away what I needed to release and uncover my natural leadership skills. My sister kept it real by revealing her inner struggles. For the first time, I was able to take my siblings off a pedestal. It was such a relief! I recognized that I wasn't the only one who had insecurities that made me diminish myself.

My boss/mentor taught me the importance of being authentic. She said two things to me that have stuck with me for over 40 years. She said that I am a natural leader, but no one would follow me if I was angry and hard. She also said that I could never be a fly on the wall because I have a voice. My sister taught me that I was not alone and that if I didn't deal with my negative feelings about myself, I could waste years on the wrong path.

Later, I attended Dillard University on a full scholarship. My low self-esteem and lack of confidence was on full display. All the beautiful black people were there. Initially, I had a hard time and made some poor decisions, like using drugs just to fit in. My daddy passed away, and I had never reconciled my anger with him about his alcoholism. Around that time, I met a friend who was my opposite. She was as soft as I was hard. I didn't have to pretend with her, and iron began to sharpen iron. I gave her some of my hardness, and she gave me the softness and balance that I needed to continue my inner work.

I hope to motivate and help you see the value and power of finding your true inner self. To encourage you to do the work to overcome self-sabotaging behaviors. To ask yourself if you've allowed you to stand in the way of living your best life. To truly evolve, you must do your inner work so you can own your path and walk into your divine destiny, just as I have.

MY INNER WORK – YOUR GUIDE

My commitment to me began when I was sixteen. I'm here because I took my power back, literally from myself. I want to help you to take your power back. To start, no matter where you are. Today, I am truly a confident woman who embraces her skin. I have a successful career and business focused on leadership and relationships.

These three core inner work principles that have become my victory lifeline. They have helped me to love myself and to be unapologetically me. They are my gift to you!

1. **Reliance** - Develop a reliance on your spirit man. We are not that good that we can do it alone. My relationship with God is everything. To discover yourself from within, you have to spend time with just you and your spirit. That's where the whole truth lives. There you learn to accept only what's yours so you can heal from the inside out.
2. **Release** - Find a means to release your thoughts and feelings so you can cope when it gets hard. I journal every day. It's important to choose how you release so that you can revisit your thoughts and have proof of your progress or lack thereof. This allows you to validate yourself, be your own cheerleader, and hold yourself and others accountable.
3. **Relationships** – Invest time and effort to build genuine relationships. Relationships should always be reciprocal, even when they are not equal. We all need people, but I encourage you to seek discernment. Relationships that require you to diminish your voice, hide your feelings or limit your value are not a priority when you're evolving.

What was my biggest life challenge is now an integral part of my life's purpose. That fat and black girl, whose daddy would lovingly call her

I AM A VICTOR!

Fat Black is no longer bound by insecurities. I am genuinely and authentically who God intended me to be. I rarely diminish my feelings or voice. If I do, I catch myself and go back to my inner work. I now believe that I AM simply black and beautiful!

It's your time to dig deep and do your inner work, and you will come out on the other side of your challenges a Victor!

BIO

Susan Appleton, CEO of Appleton Communication, is an entrepreneur, coach, speaker and corporate training and development strategist with over 30 years of proven impact and influence in leadership and business growth. As the Soft Skills Success Coach ™, she specializes in accelerating corporate, entrepreneur and non-profit leaders to the next level of success by transforming their leadership, communication, people, and relationship skills.

Susan provides customized coaching, public speaker training, workshops and soft skills programs equipping leaders with people and relationship skills, expanded leadership capacity and excellence in communication. She is passionate about strategic messaging creating an exceptional customer experience for a business' income potential and bottom line.

A transformational speaker who engages audiences with her expertise and relatable delivery style, Susan adds value to each audience member challenging them to think and act beyond the norm.

Susan Appleton
832-600-1828
www.appletoncommunication.com
susan@appletoncommunication.com
All Social Media @appletoncommunication

DEBRA BELL-CAMPBELL

Unleash the Magical Cloak
By Debra Bell-Campbell

"There is nothing so visible than what you want to hide…"
Japanese Proverb

Can you imagine being born the eighth child of 12 siblings? Who are you? Where do you fit? I have been told there is something incredibly special about the number eight, "the eight ball," as I was affectionately called. Subsequently, the "number eight" would be symbolic of how my life story unfolds and explains my Adopting Invisibility as my superpower.

To understand what led me to adopt invisibility as my superpower, you must understand where it all started. My daddy and mommy were professional breeders. They specialized in making children. Yep, 12, to be exact. We grew up in the traditional home, whereby my mom stayed at home and my daddy got the opportunity to work full-time to support team Bell. That's right; we made up all the teams to include football, basketball, soccer, and baseball, to name a few. We even had enough players to bench.

Our home was noisy all the time, and the only way you got noticed was if you were the oldest, the youngest, the naughtiest, the nicest, or the smartest. You guessed it; I wasn't any of those. As the eighth of 12 children, I too wanted a special place, so my goal was to be the smartest of the siblings. However, my shereos, i.e., my big sisters, held "the smartest" down for years as they were all smart. It didn't stop there either; my big brothers held it for a while as well. So, "the smartest" had lost its luster by the time the "eight ball" rolled out.

Does birth order affect who we are? It did for me! It was extremely difficult for me to establish my identity. I often had those feelings of not being good enough and doubting my abilities. Those feelings grew and eventually forced me to ask, where do I fit? It is amazing how your childhood affects the way you walk through life. It challenges your perception of self and how you think others see you. There were few opportunities to shine amongst the stiff competition of a dozen children. I had many shoes to fill, yet nothing seemed to fit.

I thought invisibility was just about blending in or fading in the background, and it was not. The very essence of invisibility screamed the ability to move in and out of encounters without being noticed. This magical cloak was my superpower. I finally recognized that I was not hiding from anyone. Everyone could see, except me. Finding my voice would merely be a matter of timing.

I am a victor over "Invisibility." You see, that timing was thrust upon me without warning. It would be a journey that I will never forget. It was eight months after my mother's ascension; my dad was gone just like that. It was Friday, August 7, 2015, to be exact, and nothing felt so special about the number eight. Every year, I would take my son down to the country for the summer so that he could spend time with his grandparents, as well as his aunts, uncles, and cousins. But this year would be our first summer without mom and our last with dad. I arrived at my childhood home the night before and could not wait to see my daddy, son, and everyone else. I rushed into the house and went straight to my daddy's bedroom, where he was lying on the bed facing the wall. At first, I thought he was asleep, so I ran to greet him, and he never moved. Immediately, I noticed this was different as I called out to him, "hey daddy," and kissed him on his cheek. He replied, "Hey there," yet never turned to face me. I asked if he was okay, and he said yes. I continued to make small talk and soon exited the room.

I AM A VICTOR!

The next day, I sprang to my feet as I heard my sister Carol's chilling scream. I ran into the living room, where I saw my dad slumped in his favorite rocking chair. The house was noisy, and I could not hear myself think, yet my training kicked in. I immediately told Carol to call 911, yelled to another sister to take all the kids across the street, then instructed my nephews to get my dad out of the chair and onto the floor. There, I performed CPR on my dad until emergency services arrived.

As a certified American Heart CPR instructor for years, I knew he was gone way before the Paramedics arrived, and I kept doing cycles of 30 compressions and two breaths. As I continued to breathe life into him, I begin to have flashes of all the times we laughed together, and most of who I am is him. I felt the urgency to resuscitate my own life. At that moment, I realized that I couldn't' hide anymore. I was the first one to experience my father's last breath. Yet, this was the first time in my life; I felt like I showed up when it mattered the most. I was visible!

Letting go of my invisibility cloak/superpower was overwhelming. Nevertheless, it was time as I no longer wanted to hold back. It was time to utilize the skills that I had developed throughout my life. You see, growth begins with awareness. Because I am inquisitive, I developed skills that enabled me to hear what others weren't saying. These skills enabled me to choose a profession that would serve me well for years. I got the opportunity to help others challenge their perception of self and ironically help me to "show up."

How did I conquer this sense of invisibility? I was always taught to work hard, so my work ethic trickled an avalanche of worker bee adjectives, you know, hardworking, dependable, team player, and reliable. All the terms that describe a "good employee." A good employee who really didn't talk much growing up as a member of team Bell and who would have heard me anyway.

As a counselor, I probed and encouraged my clients to do most of the talking. Fortunately, I was able to worker bee my way into harnessing my skills and promoting up. Here, I discovered people who helped to bring out the best in me. Never underestimate the power of connecting and actively listening. It was during this time my voice began to take form. I learned to embrace all the things that made me uniquely quiet, resulting in ridding myself of the magical cloak.

My leap into leadership catapulted when I connected to people living in their divine assignment, and it was always on display. Their energy was magnetic and infectious. These synchronistic encounters completely changed my idea of being (feeling) invisible.

The idea of invisibility is to not be visible, heard, or acknowledged. So, I had to make the **S.H.I.F.T**. (Stop Hiding Inside and Face Your Truth). I discovered the art of training and developing others. This mindset allowed me to recognize that I had the power to emerge as a fearless leader who utilized silence as a skill to develop powerful relationships with others.

Moreover, listening to others tell you that "you are not good enough" results in self-doubt that will paralyze your dreams. I can assure you that you can advance even if you are not the most talkative person in the room or if you are not the first person to blurt out the answers, and even if you are a quiet observer. Let me invite you to join the "introverted one," and let's make the **S.H.I.F.T.** Facing your truth is about understanding the many facets of you. Have you ever been passed over, disregarded, dismissed, or overlooked as a leader in your personal or professional life? Here are three strategies to increase your visibility and make the **S.H.I.F.T.**

- **Stand true to being authentically you.** Sometimes the true superpower is listening and observing. Knowing when to speak and when to listen. Believe you can instead of faking it until you make it.

29

I AM A VICTOR!

- **Connect effectively.** There is a stronger correlation to clarifying a message when you connect with people and not just communicate in a large or small group, via email, or text. Showing up and executing is half the battle.
- **Set your goals and never lose sight of your vision.** Submerge yourself into the culture and keep a pulse on your journey to your destination.

In conclusion, these are only a few strategies to help you unleash your magical cloak. What if I could teach you five ways to challenge your B.S. (Belief System) and set goals to align with advancing to your next level? I urge you to join me in a community of like minds and inspired Vision **S.H.I.F.T** ers. Let's usher you into your next. Make the **S.H.I.F.T** @ www.facebook.com/groups/visionshifters/.

BIO

As one of the most sought after introverted women leadership experts, Debra Bell-Campbell is a MBTI Certified Practitioner, National Certified Counselor, Wellness Strategist, Master Life Coach, Author, and Dynamic Speaker. With over 15 years of coaching women in leadership in private and corporate settings, she has designed, developed, and delivered exceptional programs to enhance professional and personal growth. She is passionate about helping her clients revel in their success in a "true to you" nature by embracing the mind and body connection. Ultimately, every client must **S.H.I.F.T**- (Stop Hiding Inside, & Face Your Truth). Did we mention Debra has designed and delivered programs for The National Weather Service and various State Departments in Florida?

Finally, as an introverted co-leader in her own home, the **S.H.I.F.T** embraces the superhero within and garner solutions. Raising a 14-year-old Prince ain't easy!

Contact her at dbellcampbell@yahoo.com, www.debrabell-campbell.com, or 904.608.2779.

OLENTHIA R. BOARDLEY

FROM DYSFUNCTIONAL TO DETERMINED
By OLENTHIA R. BOARDLEY

"Be a rainbow in someone else's cloud"
Maya Angelo

It's 8:00 am, and school has already started for the early morning children who arrive to receive free breakfast. If your family qualified for the school's subitized programs based on your family's financial income, then you qualify for free breakfast and free lunch. Well, my family did, so there I was, standing in line to get my breakfast. You would be surprised how many of us qualified for the free breakfast and lunch program. You would also be surprised how many did not register for the free breakfast and lunch program because of the shame and embarrassment of being qualified for the program. Many children just went hungry. For most, these meals would be the only meals they would get throughout the day. We have completed breakfast, and we are now being ushered to our classroom, where we hurry and put our coats in our assigned cubbies and take our seats at our desks. The day starts with taking attendance, then we all stand and recite the Pledge of Allegiance to the Flag. "I pledge allegiance to the flag of the United States of America." Wow! We had to memorize and say all the words right, or you would be called out. The teacher would make you recite the Pledge in front of the entire class. So, I made sure I was loud and strong with my delivery. Now it was time for the class to be divided into various groups as we moved around inside our classroom. The phonics station, science, math, and reading were all completed before it was time for lunch hour. I truly enjoyed all the subject stations except when it came to the reading station. Before being in your assigned reading group,

32

you were given several literacy tests to determine your grade level for reading. Unfortunately, your reading group was labeled A, B, C, D, with A being the highest for the most skilled readers and D being the lowest for the slow readers. You see where I am going with this. Well, I was placed in the D level reading group. When it was time to rotate in the classroom to another station in class, the teacher would call out which reading group would be meeting at the reading station. When the D reading group was called, the other students would laugh and say things about us, which was very hurtful. This was one reason I did not like my D reading group. While in the group, each person would have to read out loud four sentences and explain to your group what you just read and how it related to the story we were reading. As it got closer for my turn to read, the room began to spend. Sweat started to move down my back, and then I broke out into a cold sweat with water streaming on the side of my face. I thought I was going to pass out!

The teacher called, "Olenthia!" Her voice broke me out of my daze, "please read paragraph four and start on line six, then tell us about what you just read," she continued. I was in third grade, from elementary on this scene played over and over again throughout my school years. I tried my best to focus really hard on the words I was reading. I started to read, but the letters started to move and became jumbled. I could hear myself speaking; I was struggling to get the words out of my mouth. I stopped twice and started over. Calming myself down and blocking out the sounds of my classmates laughing at me. I was able to finish reading the three sentences. This was only possible because I had read ahead to find out what part I would have to read aloud. I was determined to complete my sentences, so I memorized my sentences. Therefore, able to read past the words that were moving or appeared backward. I was able to complete my assignment. Because of this dysfunction with reading, I was always placed in a lower reading group. I was said to be a slow learner because of my reading literacy. I was retained in the fifth grade for not reading on a standard reading level. I was so hurt and broken by this and did not understand what to do about my dysfunction. My second fifth-grade teacher Mrs. Fawcett was the one who gave me hope, encouragement, and determination. Mrs. Fawcett gave me tools on how to overcome my reading and comprehension dysfunction. With her guidance, I begin to improve and learn how to adjust my thinking, mind, and attitude to process my dysfunction. I did not discover what my dysfunction was until almost completing high school. IT'S IDENTIFIED AS DYSLEXIA. I have learned over the years how to manage my Dyslexia. Yes, sometimes I still get frustrated when I have to stop and refocus. With the tools I have learned and the determination not to let this dysfunction hold me back from achieving anything I put my mind to. My processing time is different from someone else; however, I still get the job done and conquer. Many people with Dyslexia are creative and bright and may be gifted in math, science, or the arts. Some even have successful writing careers. That would be me!

Dyslexia, also known as a reading disorder, is characterized by trouble with reading despite normal intelligence. Different people are affected to different degrees. Problems may include:

- Difficulties in spelling words.

- Reading quickly.

- Writing words. "

- Sounding out" words in the head.

- Pronouncing words when reading aloud.

- Understanding what one reads.

Often these difficulties are first noticed at school. People with Dyslexia have higher rates of attention deficit hyperactivity disorder (ADHD), developmental language disorders, and difficulties with numbers. Dyslexia is believed to be caused by the interaction of genetic and environmental factors. Some cases run in families. Treatment involves adjusting teaching methods to meet the person's needs. While not curing the underlying problem, it may decrease the degree or impact of symptoms. Dyslexia is the most common learning disability and occurs in all areas of the world. It affects 3–7% of the population; however, up to 20% of the general population may have some degree of symptoms. While Dyslexia is more often diagnosed in men, it has been suggested that it equally affects men and women.

Causes (But Not Limited To)

- While the exact cause is unknown, possible causes are family history.
- Premature birth or low birth weight of the baby.
- Exposure to alcohol or drugs such as nicotine during pregnancy.
- Infection that alters development of the brain in fetus.

Symptoms (But Not Limited To)

- Delay in speech Issues recalling or naming letters, numbers, and colors
- Trouble learning Misspells words

Treatments (But Not Limited To)

Treatment for children: Understand that letters and strings of letters represent these sounds and words (phonics). Comprehend what he or she is reading. Read aloud to build reading accuracy, speed, and expression (fluency). If available, tutoring sessions with a reading specialist can be helpful for many children with Dyslexia. If your child has a severe reading disability, tutoring may need to occur more frequently, and progress may be slower.

Treatment for adults: Seek evaluation and instructional help with reading and writing, regardless of your age. Ask about additional training and reasonable accommodations from your employer or academic institution under the Americans with Disabilities Act.

How I manage my Dyslexia that my help you too

1. Don't compare yourself with other people.

2. Take your time-As you allow yourself to take your time, you'll end up with a better grasp of the material.

3. It's okay to be different-Sometimes you need to sit down for an hour or so to organize your ideas before writing. Also, it's okay to start in the middle of a project and organize your ideas later.

4. Take advantage of high focus intervals – I have a higher quality of focus in the early morning hours. When you're in the "zone," take advantage of it and keep working—power through.

5. Find a quiet place to do work - It sounds so simple but having a quiet place to work makes all the difference. That way, anxiety goes down because you know where everything is and don't have to reorient yourself to a new environment.

6. Stop taking notes on every detail – Having Dyslexia makes it hard to filter information, especially when taking notes. Stop worrying about taking notes on every little thing and only jot something down if you think you need to explore the topic on your own.

7. Rely on logic instead of memorization-I rely heavily on memorization, especially during tests. Relax. If you come to a question you don't particularly remember reading about, use logic to answer the question.

It is possible to conquer your dysfunction!

BIO

Olenthia R. Boardley is the Chief Business Officer of Orbs Royal Treatment. Since 1997, Mrs. Boardley has designed and produced numerous business and wedding events. Mrs. Boardley is a Certified Wedding Planner and Leadership Team Member with The Association of Bridal Consultants, MD/DC Chapter. Mrs. Boardley is a Certified Sandals Specialist managing Caribbean business, group, and leisure conferences. Mrs. Boardley designs Caribbean honeymoons and weddings on all Sandals properties. Mrs. Boardley holds a B.S. in Business and Information Management. Mrs. Boardley's company honors the inclusion of marriage equality for all couples. Mrs. Boardley reaches out to and mentors aspiring events professionals as the Outreach Chairperson for the MD/DC Chapter for The Association of Bridal Consultants. Mrs. Boardley enjoys family life in Maryland. Mrs. Boardley is the author of "Moving At The Speed of Me" and Co-Author of "Courageous Enough to Launch."

To learn more, visit: http://www.orbsroyaltreatment.com
https://www.sandals.com/groups/business/
Email: info@orbsroyaltreatment.com
Call: 301-346-2884

I AM A VICTOR!

LINDA CALDWELL-BOYKIN

FORGET WHAT THEY SAID! YOU'RE MORE THAN ENOUGH!
BY LINDA CALDWELL-BOYKIN

"I am fearfully and wonderfully made" (Psalms 139:14). This was the scripture that changed my entire belief system about who I was. Since I can remember, I grew up with a negative perception of myself. I heard the cliche "sticks and stones can break my bones; but words can never hurt you," but I say, "sticks and stones can break my bones, but words can kill your spirit." Death and life are in the power of the tongue (Proverbs 18:21 KJV). After numerous encounters with others who spoke negative words over my life that took root in my spirit. These negative words would taint my belief system and become the foundation that would shape my identity. I was made to feel like I was not good enough or lacked what was necessary to fit in among my peers. Ultimately these experiences caused me to seek love and acceptance in all the wrong places. These unhealthy thoughts of myself not only damaged my identity but shattered my self-worth and self-esteem. The root of rejection wreaked havoc in my life, and I didn't like myself, and self-rejection became my reality. I made many sacrifices and compromises, desperately trying to be accepted by people, which came with a hefty price tag. This was a painful place to be in, and I needed relief, which led to a lifestyle of substance abuse that would progress over 15 years. My recreational use of marijuana with my peers created a sense of belonging; although the connection was unhealthy, it provided validation that I desired and longed for.

Overtime my substance abuse intensified and blossomed into a full-on battle with illicit drugs and the lifestyle that supported it. I lived to use and used to live, constantly seeking that euphoric feeling that ultimately became a way to escape from the realities of my perception of myself. This destructive cycle escalated into a rock bottom experience that introduced me to marketing and selling street pharmaceuticals (illicit drugs) to support my habit. Needless to say, after years of operating under these conditions manifested the tragic outcome of serving a prison sentence of twenty months to five years. I was mentally, emotionally, and financially broken. Everything appeared hopeless, with no way to escape. The lack of understanding who I was, the negative words of others spoken over my life manifested an outcome that would forever change my life.

Maybe you have experienced the sting of rejection by others that caused you to feel like you're not enough. Maybe you've walked through life trying to be everything to everybody so that you can be accepted. Maybe people-pleasing has become your identity with no return on your investments. Let me take a moment to encourage you not to give up and don't throw in the towel. You have what it takes on the inside of you to discover your significant value despite the misfortune. Can I solidify that you are not enough? YOU ARE MORE THAN ENOUGH!

I remember the day I received my sentence like it was yesterday. The feelings of uncertainty and fear overtook my very soul. I had never encountered incarceration, at least not for a long period. It was always an in and out process, a day here, two days there, and then released. Unfortunately, this time my stay would be much longer than I anticipated. I felt numb inside, speechless, without hope, and destitute. How in the world was I going to make it? What was going to happen to me? So many unanswered questions flooded my mind, coupled with pain and anger toward myself. Little did I know that it would be the turning point of my life and become the foundation for many VICTORIES TO COME! You may be dealing with some circumstances that have you second-guessing if you will survive. The cell walls of shame, failure, and guilt may be closing in on you, screaming you will not make it. Can I reassure you that God has a plan; to turn your tragedy into triumph. You're on the brink of a break-through.

Eventually, I settled into the throws of serving my sentence, but something within kept nudging me to get up; life was not over—enough of sitting around feeling sorry for myself and wallowing in self-pity. I could embrace being the victim, or I could rise and become the VICTOR. I decided that life's pitfalls would not become my permanent destination. Shortly after that, I was transferred to Alderson, West Virginia, where I would complete my sentence. After careful consideration, I sought a position on the campus to begin supporting myself. I landed a position cleaning the chapel, and the pay was out of this world. Are you sitting down? The hourly wage was eleven cents per hour. Oh well, I had to start somewhere; I was willing to submit to the process that would catapult me into new beginnings that could lead to a brighter future. This was what I needed to begin the process of rebuilding, repairing, and restructuring my life.

Serving in this capacity allowed me to reevaluate my life. This humbling experience was a breath of fresh air for me regardless of the pay. Considering that I had been unemployed for years, it gave me the incentive to change my trajectory. Over time, between setting the bibles in place for the other inmates and keeping the chapel clean for services, I got saved. As I began to build my relationship with Christ and read the bible; I stumbled on this scripture "I will praise thee; for I am fearfully and wonderfully made," and for the first time in my life; I knew that I was not only enough but more than enough. Finally, what I was searching for was found in Christ and not in people! Sometimes the very tragedies and traumas we face can lead us into a closer relationship with God.

Meanwhile, it was a struggle meeting the provisions needed every month because of the lack of monetary funds. At that moment, I was determined never to allow someone to dictate and control my financial freedom. Therefore, I decided to utilize my skills as a stylist to make up the difference where I lacked. I began marketing my hairstyling services to the other inmates on campus as a trade-off for other goods (deodorant, food, lotion, soap, etc.). This resurrected my passion and love for cosmetology and the desire to complete my education in that field. Having dropped out of high school due to my substance abuse, I proceeded to obtain my GED while there. Something awakened on the inside of me that impacted my soul. I started to feel empowered. Maybe you have given up on some dream because life's difficulties have handcuffed you and caused you to believe it's impossible. This does not have to be your permanent outcome! You have everything you need on the inside of you to rise up and build upon what you have left.

Finally, I completed eighteen months of my sentence was released back into society. In my reflection, I realize what should have been my demise became my springboard to turning my life totally around. Upon release, I went on to complete five years of parole without incident. To my surprise, my parole officer recommended me for a position with the D.C. Department of Corrections (God's Got Jokes) as she was impressed with my resilience and determination to make strides to rebuild my life. Thankfully, I accepted the position and worked there for several years. I had come a long way from eleven cents per hour. However, there was still that fire burning down on the inside of me that was kindled in prison to pursue cosmetology. I enrolled in Dudley's Beauty College to finish what I started years ago. Immediately upon receiving my license, I turned in my resignation and became a full-time hairstylist. After seven successful years in cosmetology, I pursued a real estate career, as another stream of income currently licensed in Maryland and D.C. In February of 2010, I became the proud owner of Salon Spirit, a spiritual haven where women can relax, renew, and be restored.

If my story resonates with you and rejection, people-pleasing, identity crisis, self-worth, self-confidence, and issues seeking acceptance from people, I got you. You are not what they said! God wants to give you beauty for ashes. Here are a few steps you can take to begin your process immediately: Relinquish all negative self-talk by speaking positive affirmation to yourself; daily, Re-define how you see yourself by looking through the eyes of God, Re-build self-confidence by learning to love yourself, and Reestablish at least three short-term goals you want to complete and commit to them. Apply these few practices, believe, and embrace that no matter what they said, "You Are More Than Enough." Go and be GREAT!

BIO

Linda Caldwell-Boykin is an entrepreneur in Maryland. She is the proud owner of Salon Spirit, LLC, where she operates as the Senior Cosmetologist since 2010. She has accomplished great success in transforming lives with creative looks for over 20 years. Her profession has served as a catalyst for a greater purpose; for those who have been broken and shattered by life darkest moments. She is known for engaging conversations that inspire individuals to propel from the ashes; and embrace their God given greatness. Linda Caldwell-Boykin obtained a Bachelor's Degree of Ministry and is currently studying for her Master's Degree in Ministry; at Virginia Bible College; in Dumfries; Virginia. Radio One recently honored and awarded 20 Pastors for their Ministry in the Community; of which she was the only woman recipient this year. When she isn't assisting others to navigate through life; she enjoys spending time with her husband. You can reach her at Ambassador4Christlcb@gmail.com

TERALEEN R. CAMPBELL

DOWNSIZED TO THE RIGHT SIZE
BY TERALEEN R. CAMPBELL

9,869 – that is the number of days I lent my time, intellect, energy, and talent to the same employer. The last 83 of those days were foggy. I had been informed that the division, of which I was the Director, was being eliminated. All of my team members and I would need to find new positions to remain with the company. In a nutshell, after 26 years of climbing the corporate ladder, I was being, as they say, downsized.

DULY NOTIFIED
I felt as though I had been gut-punched after being notified. My boss gave me the option of informing my team immediately or allowing him to do so. I opted to let him tell them because the decision was not mine, and quite honestly, I still was in a state of shock.

I successfully decreased my department's unnecessary expenses and increased efficiency, a necessity in the corporate world. During the previous budget year, the difficult decision was made to eliminate our last part-time position. I recall that meeting. We both were crying by the end. This young lady initially came as a summer intern after high school. She had now completed her undergraduate degree and was in dental school.

The most gratifying part of our discussion was her stating that my employing her for six years enabled her to obtain her degree debt-free. We do not always grasp how giving someone an opportunity can yield a great impact.

Having been through a downsizing with my previous employer, I had a frame of reference to draw upon. I noticed several loose ends. Therefore, I asked questions.

What was the exact date of closure?

Was there a severance package?

When does health insurance end?

Would my team have priority for internal positions?

I also noticed that we had not received a written notification of closure.

A Human Resource representative was not present to discuss employment options.

Initially, we were told that the closing date had not been determined, everyone would be fine throughout the holidays, and not to worry. However, team members were strongly encouraged to apply for other internal positions, some of which meant long commutes and pay cuts. Some felt pressured and uneasy. I got word that some no longer trusted me because they thought I knew about the closing and kept it from them, which was not the case. All of this was surreal and unsettling. My team was falling apart, but I could do little to save them.

IT CAN HAPPEN TO ANYONE

My boss and I had a wonderful working relationship. For 18 years, I consistently received exceptional ratings on performance appraisals. He frequently conveyed that I was a well-respected part of the marketing and company's senior leadership team. I was part of annual strategic planning meetings, a trainer, and a coach across the organization. I had also led project teams and developed the company's initial social media plan.

47

I AM A VICTOR!

PUSHING THROUGH

I grew tired of the well-meaning looks of pity that came from colleagues. As time went on, I was asked, "what are they going to do with you, Tera?" I also got statements such as, "The company can't lose you. You've contributed so much." I smiled, shrugged, and replied that I was not sure, but I would be fine. The truth is, I was not sure. The faith talk was that I would be fine. I did not know how, but I trusted the Lord.

Coming to work grew harder. One by one, my team moved on. I was both happy for them and sad. Cleaning out our workspace, storage room, and lastly, my office felt like death. Having just lost my mother the previous year, this was a familiar, sad feeling.

THE PROCLAMATION AND PROMISE

During my morning prayer time on December 18, the Lord told me that my season at the company was over and I would be fine. That revelation both discouraged and encouraged me.

I asked myself if that was enough. Answer – it had to be. My prayer shifted to God, keep me until I get to the place you have for me.

Lord, you know that I am a creature of habit. This is simply too much change. This is a bit much! Alas, I made it through the past year, so I trust you now.

MOVING ON

That first few days after my departure were like scheduled days off. Lord knows I needed the time to relax. However, after the second week, it hit me hard... I did not have a job! To repeat, I was single, in my late 40s, and unemployed!!

I did not realize it then, but depression was knocking at my door. I had money, but no job, no team to lead and see daily. My type-A leader, people-loving personality deemed this as problematic. I felt a sense of purpose in my job, mentoring, coaching, and developing teams. Now that was over. Isolated, lonely, and down are the best descriptions.

PIT STOPS

Shortly after putting my resume online, I was offered a contract position. It seemed to be perfect. Unfortunately, the work environment was very toxic. At the end of the contract, I was offered the position permanently but declined.

Within 30 days, I was offered a position with a large company. While the commute was an hour each way, the company had a great reputation. Six months later, I accepted an offer with my current employer after being contacted by someone who knew my background.

God blessed me with an upgrade in employment during a pandemic!! In addition to the salary, I am part of a work culture conducive to my lifestyle and permits telework, which helps me remain healthy. I am using my skills within a growing company and developing new ones. I can remain professional without suits and heels every day.

THE RIGHT SIZE

At this point, I see how downsizing was purposeful and yielded other victories. Did being told that I was not part of something so meaningful hurt? Absolutely, because I expected to retire there. However, had there not been a major upheaval, I would not have left. I turned down other job offers over the years. God knew that. He orchestrated it so that I was removed from my comfort zone and thrown into unchartered territory.

In retrospect, there comes a time when we need to downsize to make room for something greater, newer, emerging, and more beneficial to our future. We must trade the now for the next. I went through a period of self-discovery and self-evaluation. The aftermath of the downsizing resulted in me second-guessing myself, my decisions, and my loyalty.

I AM A VICTOR!

Despite all of that, I came through!! God has shown Himself to be a keeper and provider.

REFLECTIONS

In the end, I concluded that I had done my best. One of the most gratifying things was receiving a text message from a former assistant manager. He wrote was that the division did not close due to my failure or lack of leadership. After reading, I cried. That text was like medicine on a wound on the part of my spirit that I did not know was still aching. One victory that I have achieved is over past norms. It was previously normal to secure a good job and work for the company until you retire. While I will be a dedicated employee, I vow not to spend more time building someone else's legacy and neglecting mine.

Note: downsizing is not limited to the workplace. It can come in varying forms: change in residence, change in familial/relationship status, change in income, or change in health.

Tips as you downsizing to the right size in life:

1. **Evaluate your life.** Is it too crowded or cluttered? Watch the Lord show what you need to downsize.
2. **Evaluate the personnel-those who play key roles.** Do they still add value? This does not necessarily mean people no longer matter; rather, the roles have shifted. Minimize contact with those who will bring you down.
3. **You are likely vulnerable.** Strive to maintain positive connections.
4. **Assess your mental health.** Are you on the verge of burnout?
5. **Stay connected to God and the things of God.** (Prayer, worship, the Word) See Colossians 4:2 NLT
6. **Listen to God for the next steps**, and do not be afraid to reinvent yourself.
7. **Get some positive affirmations and read at least one out loud each day.**

8. **Maintain your character and integrity.** Psalms 41:12 tells us that God upholds us based on integrity.
9. **Build strong networks** – people looked out for me in several and sometimes unexpected ways. I was glad that I closed doors but did not burn bridges.
10. **Review your life's mission.** Are your actions and activities in alignment with your mission?

This has been a season wherein I have come to know God in quite a different way. It has been challenging yet amazing. My life is properly sized.

BIO

An award-winning author, speaker and certified coach, Minister Teraleen R. Campbell serves and intercedes on behalf of the needs of God's people. Her ministry extends to Zeta Phi Beta Sorority, Inc. She authored the sorority's Centennial Prayer and facilitated the Global Day of Prayer.

A survivor of childhood domestic abuse, at the hands of her stepfather, Teraleen is a tireless advocate against domestic violence. She participates in events which address this issue. Her community involvement has garnered recognition from professional, faith-based, and non-profit organizations.

No stranger to providing encouragement through the written word, Teraleen has co-authored several books in addition to the award-winning From Carefree to Caregiver in 2018. She created Caregivers Connect online support group. Her newest release Embracing Your New Normal Devotional provides support after the loss of a loved one.

Website - Teraleencampbell.com
Facebook, Twitter & Instagram - Teraleen Campbell

I AM A VICTOR!

Dr. Elizabeth A. Carter

L.E.A.P. With the Strength of Your 'D'NA
By Dr. Elizabeth A. Carter

*You cannot change the circumstances, the seasons, or the wind, but
you can change yourself...*
Jim Rohn

What shapes you is not just the DNA you inherit from your parents. It
is also the psychological, mental, and financial picture they paint for
you during your impressionable childhood years. The canvas captures
the shining sun of a joyous union, the blue sky of contentment, and the
storms of discipline. My framed painting was of a young, married
couple with two children in a modest home in a diverse part of
suburban New York.

Over time, that myopic picture of life changed. Unfortunately, that lack
of foresight did not resonate with me until a hospital visit in 1987. Not
looking up from a bed but looking down at my mother, who was
admitted for a stroke. I stared down at her tired eyes, drooping lip on
the right side, intravenous needles in her arms, and tubes in nearly
every orifice of her body. My subconscious mind asked me, "Is this it?
Do I now have to support the family financially?" I was fighting back
the tears, and my heart started beating faster. I was a sophomore in
college, commuting to the local university; my brother was a high
school senior. My 10-hour a week job was not going to be able to pay
a mortgage, utilities, and whatever other debts my mother had procured
during the years. That day was the culmination of the D's not in my
DNA; Divorced, Dependent, Degreeless, and possibly, Disabled.

PARENTAL DNA

My Dad was an only child born in Trinidad to a 'Tiger Mom.' For those not familiar, the Tiger Mom moniker was given to mothers who pushed their children to high achievement levels, typical of Chinese and East Asian cultures. Caribbean cultures also embodied this trait, as evidenced by my Dad's high expectations of my brother and me. 'Caribbean Dad,' I will rename him, was educated and an educator. I was fortunate that the complete tiger mentality was not inherited, as my constant delivery of a report card with many B's and few A's would have had more severe consequences. The conversations about college only had one set of options, which institution would add Elizabeth to their alumni list.

My mother was a caregiver at heart. The eldest of four girls, her parents were from the south, where homeschooling was the norm. Her mother had a GED, her father's actual grade of completion unknown. 'Caregiver Mom' graduated from high school and went to work for the phone company. She was intelligent and sharp. After my brother and I were born (three years apart), she became a full-time housewife. Her amazing talent was that she could nurture with one hand and discipline with the other hand at the same time.

My parents' DNA provided the gift of intelligence, analytical aptitude, and humility. I also inherited nasal trouble, high cholesterol, the risk of heart disease, and possible colon cancer. Sickle-cell trait and thyroid problems skipped a generation and hit me. These genetic hand-me-downs are easily recorded and monitored with tests. The D's not in my DNA were not ones that were expected or remedied with medication.

FOUR D'S NOT IN MY DNA: DIVORCED, DEPENDENT, DEGREELESS, AND DISABLED.

In 1980, my parents announced that they were getting divorced. I was distraught and confused. There were no fights, arguments, or signs of discontent that I could remember. Caribbean Dad had already taken a job out of state. Caregiver Mom's facade did not seem affected. Her

I AM A VICTOR!

children were her priority. She was to run the household with the same force and focus as before.

Yet, finances seemed different. I was too young to understand the severity, but I could sense a change. Caregiver Mom had to find a job, which was a difficult task. First, she did not drive. She grew up in the city with public transportation, and our suburban amenities were within walking distance. Second, without a college degree, decent-paying jobs were limited. After securing a car and employment, with alimony and child support, I thought we were all right. Over time, I could tell the bills versus paydays' timing indicated that we were living 'paycheck to paycheck.' In those days, you did not ask questions; that was grown folk's business, and whatever arrangements were in the divorce decree were not my cross to bear.

As my heart rate regained a normal pace in that hospital room in 1987, it now felt like it was my cross to bear. If Caregiver Mom is permanently disabled from this stroke, I become the caregiver. If she could not maintain the household with a job, how could we survive with just disability income? Fortunately, the stroke was mild enough that she was able to resume most of her normal activities. But there was some permanent brain damage. When I would ask how she was doing, Caregiver Mom would always say, "I'm doing good, I'm fine." Five words she still utters to this day in response to the same question, regardless of her true feelings.

I knew we were not fine in 1990 when we had to pack and move with little notice. The actual reason was not disclosed to me at the time, but I assume it was a mutual agreement between Caregiver Mom and the bank. My memories of love, life, happiness, and sadness were now involuntarily boxed in a storage unit.

TAKING MY 'D'NA AND LEAPING INTO A NEW PAINTING
Charles R. Swindoll said, "Life is 10% what happens to you and 90% how you react to it". My mother's reaction to being Divorced,

Dependent, Degreeless, and Disabled could have been depression, drinking, or drugs. Refusing to let these four D's crush my life, I vowed to create a new psychological, mental, and financial picture. While Caribbean Dad and Caregiver Mom gave me D's and DNA that were not optimal, they gave me the care, character, and courage to change my life's canvas. With that strength, I leaped into a painting with a shining sun of Dreams, the blue sky of Destination, the storms of Disappointment, with white clouds of Determination. My L.E.A.P. matrix contains actions and affirmations that allowed me to move forward. I share a set of them here.

L- Let go and go live. This is easier said than done, and I am a work in progress. When my parents divorced, I was 13, evolving into a young woman. Just as I was becoming curious about boys, my thoughts about marriage and relationships changed. My tiger intuition told me there would not be a man good enough for me in Caribbean Dad's eyes. He always remained active in my life, but rarely did I introduce him to my boyfriends. Living my life trying to please him, wanting to be better than the B's I gave him as a child, I engrossed myself in my education and career.

E- Educate yourself; knowledge is power. Despite graduating with a bachelor's degree, that alone was not a guarantee of lifetime cash flow. I was determined to be competitive in the corporate environment, especially with minority women fighting for equal pay. My childhood B's turned into graduate A's. I obtained two master's degrees, an insurance designation, and a Ph.D. My career achievements in finance provided salaries to create my financial independence. The 1987 tears and fears of financially supporting the family are now non-existent.

A- Allow only temporary setbacks. These achievements were not completed without challenges. There were years when I was living paycheck to paycheck, stored my possessions in a storage unit, slept on Caregiver Mom's couch, and relied on others for transportation. History was repeating itself. Yet, the paintbrushes of hope and perseverance always kept my life's picture illuminated. I started my first master's degree but had to stop due to financial constraints. Years later, when I recovered with a new job, the school re-admitted me without penalty.

P- Prioritize what you can control. Caregiver Mom is my reminder of my medical and hereditary history. Since 1987, she has had two more major strokes, a mechanical valve and pacemaker implanted, takes nine different medications, and was recently diagnosed with dementia. As her caregiver now, I am very aware that the next 911 call could result in a fifth D not mentioned in this story. I insist that all my medical appointments, ultrasounds, mammograms, colonoscopies, blood work, and medication refills are completed like clockwork.

My LEAP may be regarded as avoidance to some and overcompensating to others, but this solution worked for me. Regardless of your DNA pain, may these words allow you to leap into your new painting.

Bonus: More of the L.E.A.P. matrix
>   **L**- Live within your means.
>   **E**- Embrace an 'act today' mentality.
>   **A**- Ask for relief, reprieve, or re-start.
>   **P**- Put purposeful people in your path to guide you.

BIO
Dr. Elizabeth A. Carter is a finance leader, speaker, trainer, and author. With over 25 years working in Corporate settings, Dr. Carter's unique combination of financial acumen and knowledge empowerment has provided her the opportunity to lead, mentor and develop others in both profit and non-profit organizations.

In 2016, she started AAPPEAL, LLC, a company branded on her "Absolute Passion for Performance, Engagement, Analytics, and Leadership." Women who feel unseen in the workplace coach with her when they are ready to make their voice visible. She empowers them with tips, tools, and resources that illuminates their presence, and increases the profits of their organization. Finding this passion provided her the platform to share her gift with others and continue her finance career.

Dr. Carter holds a PhD in education specializing in training and performance improvement.

Ready to LEAP personally and/or professionally?
Website: https://www.eac-aappeal.com
Facebook, Twitter, Instagram – eacaappeal

I AM A VICTOR!

SONYA CARTER

I'M OVER IT

BY SONYA CARTER, EMPOWERMENT PURPOSE COACH, PREACHER, AND SPEAKER

"Your words don't carry enough weight to stop God's plans for my life."
Sonya Carter

A few years ago, these words resonated with my spirit. I finally got it. I finally was able to free myself from the opinion of others and what they thought about me. I no longer participated in being held hostage to what I thought people were saying about me or what I knew they said about me and had to act as if I didn't know. The truth of the matter is YES, those negative words stung, and yes, those words hurt, but those words could not hinder me unless I gave life to the words spoken.

You see, I was used to being talked about. Just a little background at 13 years old, I was raped. I had to walk past one of my rapist's house to get home from school. So, every day I endured the name-calling, the belittling, and all those words that people call other people when they think they know their story. So, I learned how to navigate life through name-calling and being talked about. I knew the truth, so I let it run off me like water. Back then, I didn't even try to defend myself. I said nothing. I let people wonder.

So, when I met the man of my dreams and knew he was the one I wanted to spend the rest of my life with, I just knew everything was going to be alright. He was Christian, born and raised, and a minister of the Gospel. I was a Christian and understood I had a calling from God on my life. I just knew the universe was going to be nice and let me sail off into the sunset with my knight in shining armor. Right? Wrong! The opinion of others would not allow us to be happy. Why is that? Church people can be the most critical people. Although not said, but my perception, "I was not the kind of girl that a mother would want for her son." I had a baby, and my soon-to-be-man was a virgin. It just was not a good look for him to choose someone like me. Especially when this virgin man is the Pastor's son, it didn't stop our plans. We still got married, but it sure did complicate our life.

I went from being the "girl with a baby" to points in sermons of the "used woman who wanted a good man who saved himself." No matter how much I told myself that I knew God forgave me deep down, the struggle was real. It seemed as though I would never live it down and I would always be belittled and snickered about in some form or fashion. The truth of the matter, I did not have to contend with the comments from the people outside when it was the comments from his family on the inside that consistently pissed me off. How in the world am I supposed to overcome this, I thought to myself? I was expected to look cute and be the cute little wife on the pew. As a matter of fact, my name went from being Sonya to Kennard's wife. My becoming Mrs. Carter made me lose my identity.

Over the years, some things pushed me further to the edge, from a physical fight to being called to fruitless meetings, to having my spiritual gifts just totally ignored. You name it; I dealt with it, "all in the name of the Lord." Things finally came to a head shortly after I had my 4th child. I realized that I was worthless and could offer nothing. I sunk deeper into despair. So, I plotted my own death. Yes, you heard me right. I plotted my own death. I would sit in church, and while the sermon was going on, I would be thinking of all the ways I could kill myself. Maybe deep down, I didn't want to die as I never attempted suicide, but I sure did think about it many days. But at the time, I just wanted to die and leave my husband with the insurance money. If I had the assurance that my family would live in the state of security that we were living in, I probably would not be here today to write this story. I honestly felt like the pain would never stop, and there was no one to rescue me. After all, I was the minister's wife. There was no outlet and no one I could trust to tell how I really felt. And the Titus women that the Bible speaks about, where were they? All the shouting and speaking in tongues did not reveal to anyone that I was in TROUBLE. So, I prayed and suffered in silence. I suffered in silence and made unwise decisions while I was pressing through. But God...

I kept pressing my way to the house of the Lord and praying. Eventually, I took myself to a Christian counselor who helped me to understand my worth. From there, it was by any means necessary; I am climbing out of this pit. I am not saying this is the best method, but I am sharing my process and what worked for me. I realized that it didn't matter what other people thought about me. What matters is what God thinks about me and what I think about myself. I remember when the lightbulb turned on. And I want to share it with you because I think everyone reading this story will have a lightbulb moment in their life.

One day I was on the phone talking to my sister, Jamie. We were talking about different things that I had endured over the years in ministry when I began to cry. As tears streamed down my face, I said these words, "I'm fine just the way I am." At that moment, I realized God made me special and gave me unique giftings that only I could do. It was at that moment that I realized I was FREE. I could walk in my truth and accept the "ME" God created me to be. I realized, "Your words don't carry enough weight to stop God's plans for my life." I learned not to get caught up in the hype of what people say because many are still wearing masks that hid the real "them." I, instead, bask in the truth found within my relationship with God and who He said I am.

I leave you with this acronym as it has been my saving grace and helps me navigate my life over the years.

A -Accept who God made you to be. Your flaws, hair, skin color, body shape, wittiness, loud laugh, and antics~ all of you.

C - Change for no one except God. God is the author and the finisher of your faith. He is the creator and master architect of your life. If you allow the potter to mold you, you will be exactly who He wants you to be.

C - Care for others but not at your own expense. Evoke the power of "No." It is okay to say no and do what makes you comfortable. As long as you are following the direction of the CEO of your life (God Himself), you cannot go wrong.

E - Endeavor to follow God in everything that you do and say. People may not always understand. Heck, you may not always understand how God is leading you, but if you follow Him, you will be the warrior woman He created you to be. Remember, there are joys and benefits for walking in obedience. Don't worry about your time. Your time is in God's hands.

P - Peace over pleasure- Choose peace. It might give you pleasure to fight back and respond to everything that rubs you the wrong way, but your peace might be disturbed by doing so. Peace will keep your stress down and help you rest better at night. Choose Peace.

T - Teach others how to embrace the treasure within. When we love who God created us to be, we can walk in VICTORY. You may have to say it, or you may have to show it. Either way, each one reach one.

I am not a VICTOR because I did everything right. I AM A VICTOR because I withstood the process and allowed God to heal my heart. With God's healing came a renewed mind, restoration, and rekindled relationships. My family is now ROCK SOLID.

I AM A VICTOR!

BIO

Sonya Carter is a wife and mother who is gainfully employed in the Federal Government. She holds a Master of Arts in Discipleship Ministries and a Master of Divinity in Professional Ministries from Liberty University. Sonya is an Empowerment Purpose Coach, motivational speaker, and published author. She is the proud owner of Create2 LLC, creator of I AM THURSDAYs, and Fierce N Free Podcast. Sonya contributes her success to the faithfulness of God, her parents Sheila Hamilton and James Stieff III, and her supportive husband, M. Kennard Carter.

MARCELLA CHEEKS STRETCH

SIX THOUSAND MILES FROM HOME
BY MARCELLA CHEEKS STRETCH

Have you ever felt that no one understood why you were out of touch? You will show up at family or social events and be absent mentally— the reason they did not understand because they were not in your shoes. I heard a quote from an unknown author "Before you start to judge me, step into my shoes and walk the life I'm living, and if you get as far as I am, just maybe you will see how strong I really am." With that said, let us take a walk down memory lane together.

It was the summer of 2007 my oldest son enlisted in the U.S. Army right after high school. He left Maryland and flew to Fort Benning, Georgia. I stalked Fort Benning's Facebook pages in search of a picture of my soldier. I joined Army Mom and Army Parents Facebook groups for support. My son completed One Stop Unit Training (OSUT) in December 2007. I now have a proud Infantryman who will support and defend the United States Constitution against all enemies, foreign and domestic. I was a proud mother, yet I was on edge by the unknown. Keep in mind this was during the time Iraq and Afghanistan were hot.

My family and I attended the graduation at Fort Benning, GA. On a side note, my youngest son was in the 10th grade and an Army JROTC student. On graduation day, we had my youngest son walk around Fort Benning in his JROTC uniform, and all eyes were on him. Some people had to take a 2nd look at seeing a young teenager in uniform. By the way, my JROTC son was walking around like a General.

Moving forward, when my son returned home after graduation for a visit, we hosted a family gathering at our home. Everyone was excited to see the handsome soldier. Next was his move to his first and only duty station. It was January 2008, off to Fort Lewis he went to be a fulltime soldier. While stationed at Fort Lewis, he was over 2,000 miles from home. I learned to cope with the distance by keeping busy. Knowing that I could call my son most days gave me some peace of mind.

My journey six thousand miles away from home started in the Summer of 2009. My son was starting his deployment to Iraq. This deployment put me in a dark place. The sleepless nights, the stories on the news, and the lack of understanding from others was a lot to digest. I was going about my daily activities in a daze. My work performance decreased due to the lack of focus. I kept pressing to get things done despite the circumstances. I really believe this was the beginning of my grey hair process.

I was sitting at home one day in September 2009 and said to myself, "there must be thousands of other parents currently feeling the same way I am feeling." I cannot be alone with my thoughts and anxiety. With the encouragement of some Army parents, friends, and family, I started a Facebook group, Parents of Deployed Soldiers (PODS). As the group matured, the Admins and I agreed to change the name from Parents of Deployed Soldiers to Parents of Deployed Servicemembers. The name change allowed the group to include all branches of the military. PODS was started with a total of 5 Army Moms. Over 11 years, the group has grown to 6.5K members. My rough estimate is that over 7 thousand parents have been in the group at some point and time. Some members leave the group once their deployed troop has returned to the States, even though membership is voluntary forever.

I had no idea that PODS would evolve into a lifeline for countless parents. Just to know, instead of having a pity party about a situation that was out of my control, I decided to be proactive. The life-changing experiences have made the trip over six thousand miles from home a worthwhile trip.

The thousands of Care Packages received over 11 years melts my heart to no end. Since I am an idealistic person with a support team to assist with the execution makes me forever grateful. At the beginning of the project, we were a small group of under 400 members. We decided to exchange the names of our troops for sending Care Packages. The idea was great. Our troops received Care Packages from parents they did not know. Just to hear, "Mom, some lady in Texas sent me a Care Package" was music to my ears. Our Care Package project grew so big that we added nonprofit organizations to become senders. Our partners are Blue Star Mothers' Chapters, Honor Our Troops, N.C. Packs, Semper Fi Sisters, Girl Scouts, Boy Scouts, schools, businesses, and individuals. We used the theme "Give Thanks to a Deployed Troop" as our slogan.

How do you cope with your son having a birthday while over six thousand miles from home? You turn your sadness into gladness by showering them with birthday cards. Yes, I asked PODS, family, friends, and co-workers to mail my oldest son a birthday card for his 21st birthday. Now look at this; my son received over 300 birthday cards nationwide. The mailroom in Iraq had never seen that many birthday cards received by one soldier. I expanded the idea by creating a birthday list of all the deployed/overseas troops. Almost 11 years later, the joke overseas is "That Birthday group got you" or "You have been PODed" whenever a troop receives a bunch of birthday cards. My youngest son turned 22 while in Afghanistan. His most memorable birthday card was receiving a check for $10 in his card that he could not cash. Only because the check was written out to Denzel Washington instead of his last name, I said that happens when you share the same first name with Denzel Washington.

The stories from so many members have been extremely rewarding. To hear 3 sets of parents say, "We are cousins." Yes, three sets of parents found out they are cousins just by being in PODS. To hear parents say, "We are neighbors." To hear sets of parents say I have met my best friend in PODS; this all makes the trip six thousand miles away from home well worth the ride. The group has experienced face to face meetups. Some parents have met in person via traveling or by living near each other. I have had face to face meetups with some parents while traveling around the country for personal and business. I made sure that I took the time to meet PODS members in person by having lunch or dinner with them. I also met some local members within PODS for lunch or dinner. The highlight of meeting a group member is the warm greeting we receive from each other as if we have been friends for years.

The group has experienced its highs, lows, ups, and downs, but through it all, we are Victors. We have celebrated the Welcome Homes whenever a troop returned to their military base. We have attended welcome home ceremonies on behalf of another parent who could not travel to the home base. The welcome home signs, pictures, and videos are sent to the parents of that troop who could not have family present to welcome them home. We also are there for the Blue Star Mother, who becomes a Gold Star Mother. If possible local members of PODS attend the final service of our fallen hero. I had the honor to attend a service at Arlington National Cemetery for a PODS member who became a Gold Star Parent. In honor of our fallen hero, PODS makes a financial contribution to the charity of the family's choice. We also send a symbolic wreath to the final service on behalf of the group.

Above all, PODS is a 24/7 closed Facebook Support group for our parents. A place of refuge when struggling with deployment and other issues. Knowing there is a safe place to find comfort during a vulnerable period in life is beyond measure. Our seasoned parents remain in the group to assist and support our new members.

Roll Call! It is 3:00 am; who is awake? This very statement has brought so much comfort to the members of PODS. To know you are never alone, and we get it. The countless Thank You's for starting this awesome one of a kind group can never go unnoticed.

I thank God, my family, and my friends for lending me to thousands of people so that I can become a Victor during a rough time in my life. Remember, you can become a Victor by turning what looks like a down and out situation into a positive situation that can benefit others.

I dedicate this chapter to my Sister Vernella Cheeks, who passed suddenly the day after my oldest son returned home from his deployment to Iraq.

BIO
Marcella Stretch is a native of Washington D.C., a graduate of F.W. Ballou High School, and she received her Bachelor of Science. degree in Accounting from Shaw University in Raleigh, NC. She recently retired from the Federal Government after 37 years. Marcella currently resides in Upper Marlboro, MD with her husband Lewis. She is the mother/stepmother of five adult children and 10 grandchildren.

Marcella gives all thanks to God for allowing her to impact others. Her free time is spent volunteering with various organizations including Year Up, Military Organizations, Zeta Phi Beta Sorority, Inc., Saving Grace Animal Rescue, and her church family. She is the leader of the Parents of Deployed Servicemembers Facebook group. She inspires others to overcome their life's obstacles by being a better person, lifting as they climb.

JOYCE CHESLEY HAYWARD

FROM AIR AMBULANCE TO CLARITY
BY JOYCE CHESLEY HAYWARD

Have you ever had one of those days that changed the trajectory and perspective of your life? A day that becomes one you will always remember where you were, what you were doing, how you were feeling? Well, July 16, 2019, was that day for me. It started as an ordinary day, so I thought. I had wrapped up clients' payroll tax returns the day before, and there were a few meetings and follow-ups with clients regarding their financial matters. That afternoon, while on the phone with a client, a call came in, and I saw my husband's number on the ID.

Now, you should know that I am an entrepreneur at heart. I enjoy helping clients, and much of my business is over the phone. Whenever I was on the phone with a client, that was my sole focus. If another call came in – no matter who I saw it was – I jotted down the pertinent information to call them back. And, if you're anything like me, I might forget to go back and look at the note! I'd realize sometimes hours later that I didn't call them back. There were times I'd come across the note and, as I tapped what I felt was my bobble head, I'd apologize as I called back. It happened too often where a family member or a friend I called back much later said, "It's OK, never mind, I needed something quick at that moment." Or, worse, they said: "I called to let you know something happened to 'so and so' and I thought you wanted to know." In those moments, I felt I had let them down. More importantly, I'd let myself down.

I had begun to look at my life, the busy-ness, and my business, and I wondered: what is really important? Am I really living my best life? Where is the joy in doing all that I'm doing if I'm not present for those who are most important to me? Is there really success or victory in where I am headed? I was helping others "Maximize Profitability," but, what was I prioritizing or allowing to get lost in the quest for success? I wondered if I was really promoting the right things.

Then it happened, the event that gave me clarity. Have you ever been in a position where God has 'hit' you? That kind of event where you acknowledge if you don't get it easily, if you're too busy to listen to "God's still small voice," God will shout? My late God-fearing father used to tell me: "If you don't listen, you'll feel." Well, July 16, 2019 showed me I hadn't been listening, so God shouted, and I FELT the impact.

As I saw my husband's number come up that afternoon, "something said" (i.e., God's leading) take the call. I asked my client to hold one moment. As my husband, Gil, who is normally an upbeat, fun, and funny kind of guy, greeted me with his usual, "Hi Honee," I heard a very serious tone. Before I could even ask what was wrong, he let me know that he was leaving the doctor's office and that we needed to get to the hospital IMMEDIATELY. Gil told me the doctor had called ahead to the emergency room to take him right away due to some irregularities they found during his checkup. He told me he'd be there in about 2 minutes to pick me up. My methodical brain started tabulating questions: How is he driving, what is going on? Does this have something to do with the heartburn he had the other night? My head was spinning, as I hadn't quite grasped it all. So, I went on autopilot and grabbed my computer and a few folders, not knowing what was ahead of me. I was preparing to use any 'downtime' as is typical with emergency rooms, not comprehending; this was NOT typical. When my husband arrived, I was ready to go.

I AM A VICTOR!

During the ride to the hospital, my husband seemed fine, on the outside. But I knew he was really concerned. So, I tried to reduce my tendency to ask too many questions and just be there and listen. When we arrived at the hospital, they took my husband right away. During the numerous tests that evening, I only picked up my computer to give my husband a diversion and bring some normalcy to the abnormal situation. My computer on my lap (the "other man," as Gil called it) had become a regular occurrence, so it was something we could laugh a bit about. Later that evening, we were told my husband had a blockage in his heart and that he needed emergency surgery, which could not be done in our island home of Bermuda. The next day, we were on an air ambulance to Johns Hopkins in Baltimore for my husband to have heart surgery. I'd never ridden in an air ambulance, and I thank God the two medical attendants were jovial and friendly. But, during that ride, the gravity of the situation hit me. My mind was beginning to feel as cloudy as what I saw outside my window. I wondered: what is really happening right now? What are we headed toward? Throughout this time, I'd been praying without ceasing. As I stared out the window and heard the light banter of conversation between Gil and the attendants, I asked God to please bring us both through. After arriving in Baltimore, as Gil and I sat in the hospital room eating dinner before the surgery scheduled for the next morning, I understood it could have been our last supper. As a woman of faith, I didn't allow myself to believe that all would not go well. I believed that it was God's will for my husband to have a successful surgery and pull through. However, at that moment, I thought, you never know when the last time is the last time.

Praise God my husband came through the surgery and is doing well!! But the experience was an eye-opener. What could have been a ride through the clouds and uncertainty became, for me, an epiphany. It showed me that our lives and businesses need balance. It highlighted what is important in life and that, as important as my business is, it isn't the MOST important thing at all times. I saw it was about mindset and how I thought about my business. It was important, yes, but all important and all-encompassing: no. I thought about clients and friends in business and how many were also: working and over-working, spending countless hours in their businesses, and quite often, missing out on family events and functions.

I decided from this experience that we need to get back to the reason we are in business: to enjoy what we do. I recognized it doesn't have to be "either-or," but it should be "both-and" - profit AND life/balance/freedom. It is possible to have a passion for your business and your life. There has to be a balance between business and busy-ness. In that air ambulance ride, God gave me the clarity to see that I needed to have a business that has balance and to help others find that balance as well. So, I decided to develop the Profit Freedom program to assist business owners with this clarity. Based on biblical principles, the Profit Freedom program helps put business in alignment in all areas to help business owners to have more profit in their business for more freedom in their lives. The 7 keys to Profit Freedom can be found on our website under downloads.

In all, I want to leave you with 5 points to help you to be "C.L.E.A.R." as we consider our lives, businesses, and where we place importance.

1)   CONSIDER AND CHOOSE WHO AND WHAT IS MOST IMPORTANT IN YOUR LIFE

a.   Who will be with you, and who do you want with you in your last days?

b.   Treat them special every time you encounter them.

2)   LET GOD, YOUR FAMILY, AND LOVED ONES BE YOUR PRIORITY.

a. Prioritize key persons before your business, job, etc.; and take their calls

b. Make God THE Chairman of the Board of your Business. Our devotional can help with that: https://fusion4business.com/let-go-devotional/

I AM A VICTOR!

3)   ENLIGHTEN OTHERS TO KNOW WHAT/WHO IS MOST IMPORTANT TO YOU

a.   Let them know when those important people need you; you'll be there. At times that may mean interrupting a meeting or conversation, in an unobtrusive way.

b.   If people don't understand what's most important to you, they are not your ideal client or job; that is not the "tribe" you want to build

4)   AVAIL YOURSELF TO THOSE YOU LOVE AND CARE ABOUT. Be Present with those who are the gifts in your life.

5)   REJOICE IN EACH DAY GOD HAS GIVEN and be thankful for it!

BIO

Joyce considers herself a "transplanted Bermuda onion" after marrying her husband and leaving Maryland to live in his home of Bermuda. She is a Certified Public Accountant (CPA) and graduate of Georgetown University, as well as a member of Alpha Kappa Alpha Sorority, Inc. Joyce is a speaker, coach, consultant, and trainer. After managing a CPA firm in Maryland and holding senior positions in Government and international business in Bermuda, Joyce has launched Fusion4Business (F4B) both a US and a Bermuda Corporation. F4B helps businesses optimize their financial health and wealth and experience "Profit Freedom." Joyce is an ordained minister in the AME church with a Doctor of Divinity, and she loves to dance for the Lord. She is also blessed to have two bonus sons. Check out F4B's programs at http://www.fusion4business.comand connect on LinkedIn https://www.linkedin.com/in/joyce-chesley-hayward-a7640a80/and on FB https://www.facebook.com/joyce.v.haywardto help you "Maximize Profitability for Your Small Business"

TANIKA A. CRAIG-SPEAKS

THE DAY I WOKE UP DEAD
BY TANIKA A. CRAIG-SPEAKS

I vividly remember driving on Connecticut Avenue in Bethesda, Maryland, in rush hour traffic on my way to work. Listening to my playlist and running through my mental to-do list. I was mentally and physically exhausted. For a single moment, everything went blank and silent. Too silent, like a piercing sound in your ear. Boom! The loud crashing sound awakened me, hands still gripping the steering wheel. I pushed my eyes open and tried to regain control of the vehicle, but it was too late. I rear-ended a commercial truck and was on the verge of death, without any recollection of the accident or how I lost control of reality. I felt completely numb.

The smell of the engine burning from the cracked radiator was causing me to cough. The hood of the car smashed into the windshield. I was disoriented and started looking around to gather my whereabouts. Everything stopped, and nothing made sense. Questions began racing through my mind, did I hurt someone? Should I get out of the car? The other drivers were watching with great concern. A Police Officer nearby ran across the street to assist me. My reaction was delayed, I could see his mouth moving, but I could not hear his words. In shock, I grabbed my phone, but I did not know who to call. Shaking uncontrollably, I repeated I am ok, I'm ok. Another driver approached the car and asked, "Do you need an ambulance?" My response was again. I am ok. Everything became a blur for several hours.

Specifically, I remember being tired for so long that I could not recall having a moment to relax or even feel happy. But there was not any moment that I was exhausted like this one. After a day that seemed longer than I ever lived, I stopped to thank God that I was physically alive. This was the moment I was shown everything I needed to see about my Life. (1) I ignored the signs that I was exhausted, worrying about making my commitment to be on time for work. (2) I acknowledged that I was operating on autopilot. (3) My first reaction was to regain control car instead of pushing the brake to stop. (4) I was worried that I had injured someone along the way instead of checking to see if I was injured. (5) No one ever asked what happened, and they only wanted to know if I was ok. I vowed to be intentional to live my life to the fullest. From that day, I began to reflect on my purpose and why God saved me from death. The short answer is to be a warrior and teach people how to be resilient.

> *"Life doesn't get easier or more forgiving.*
> *We get stronger and more resilient."*
> Steve Maraboli, Life, the Truth, and Being Free

Scholars might teach about resilience and survival from definitions learned. Such as, resilience is the ability to stay strong through difficulties. Likewise, survival is the capability to be in a reasonable state in dangerous situations. In other words, fight or flight. Unfortunately, I was taught this my entire LIFE as a survivor. My story began when my mother was fifteen years old. She dared to become a mother despite my father being a drug addict and suffered from schizophrenia. The barriers that accompanied being a young girl and poverty proved to be great, but she did the best she could to carry on. Somehow, she must have known I would need the tools to be resilient.

When I was two years old, my father physically attacked me, leaving physical and emotional scars to follow me for the rest of my LIFE. He was arrested after this, resulting in him being absent most of his life. I still forgave him and saw through his problems, and I took the highest pain when he died. I was in my early 20s.

I AM A VICTOR!

My mother was always ambitious, has many skills, and is a natural problem solver. Her experiences taught me that I could figure things out and overcome any obstacles. However, she was extremely strict. My sister and I were not allowed to break the rules under any circumstances. At the same time, when I was seventeen years old, she allowed me to visit my boyfriend at Christmas. I fell asleep on the couch and missed my 11:00 pm curfew. My mother was so angry at my disobedience and stated, "If I was grown to stay out all night, don't return home." I never returned. I was months away from finishing high school. I felt lonely, but I still had my first love, who I married one year later in 1995. Like many others, this love felt right but weak, as I suffered several marital issues for years. We were teens living as adults with no guidance, which was the turning point of my resilience.

Motherhood quickly followed marriage, and now I was taking on a new, unfamiliar role before I could adjust to being a wife. Decades later, I was able to take many things out of my traumas that make me incredibly proud such as grit and hope. Being a young mother, starting at eighteen, I have raised three incredible children, and they are brilliant entrepreneurs, musicians, and college athletes. I started the first generation of high school graduates in my family and was also the first to receive an MBA. I have gone through so much, but at the same time, I have accomplished many victories that made me grateful for the journey. I learned what I truly acquired through my experiences was strength and resilience. Taking awareness of this, I started my life-changing business, Lifeshift Empowerment Group, teaching young individuals how to overcome their traumas and build strong resilience skills. Gladly, I have been able to help more than 2,000 teens find self-discovery.

Now you ask me, why was the day I almost died, the day I knew I was unstoppable? The answer is simple. It was the day I was reminded; I was alive. I remembered all that I have conquered and all of those I have helped. I knew nothing was over for me, and I would still complete incredible milestones in this cruel world I live in. I like to think we are all meant to fall only to gather ourselves back up to value each moment we have and use our lives as driving forces for tremendous success. Resilience is not about winning or losing. It is about surviving. With every word, every experience, every heartache, every trauma, and every victory, I was one step closer to becoming the person I am proud to be today, a VICTOR. It has all opened my eyes and made me realize that I am truly unstoppable.

Surviving is not about knowing what to do. It is about knowing that you may need to push yourself through experiences. I was born with this nature, and I have used it my entire LIFE. I was hurt too many times, but it was within my essence to keep fighting. I applied what I learned to protect myself and the people I love every single day. But the day I almost died; I learned the most powerful lesson about survival; I did not take enough care of myself first.

Survivalists must take care of themselves so they can take care of others. I almost gave up, but I endured every trial and tribulation through God's mercy. I started healing once more, taking that as a new beginning. My story is risky, but it is necessary. The Generations that read these words will be inspired to take the first step and be guided to victory. Knowing the tears I have cried were worth someone standing up for themselves and finding resilience is what drives me further. It makes me grateful for every turn and every step. Trauma seems unfair, but my experiences have given me an unbreakable, unshakable WILL to live. There is nothing an individual cannot overcome. You do not need permission to rescue yourself. It is the only means of survival. I am Tanika Craig-Speaks, and I show up in the world as a barrier breaker that heals.

Strategies for discovering resilience:

- Courage is a choice and willingness to confront agony, pain, danger, uncertainty, and intimidation.
- Mindset is critical to eliminate internal and external negativity, including destructive self-talk.

I AM A VICTOR!

- Believe in yourself. The things people say from their mouth is what they believe in the heart and will eventually show up in their actions. Remember, you are as capable as the next person.
- Hope is an optimistic state of mind based on the expectation of positive outcomes in one's life. "Faith shows the reality of what we hope for; it is the evidence of things we cannot see. Hebrews 11:1"
- Never give up it is not finished until it is over.

> *"Strength doesn't come from what you can do. It comes from overcoming the things you once thought you couldn't."*
> Nikki Rogers

BIO

Tanika A. Craig-Speaks is a Transformational Speaker, Entrepreneur, and Transition Coach who has devoted her work to enriching teen's and young adults' lives. Her fusion of real-life stories and hands-on activities allows her to connect with her audience at an individual, fun, and intense level.

As the Founder of Lifeshift Empowerment Group, Tanika creates a safe space for young people to be engaged and supported while overcoming the challenges of transitioning into young adulthood. She partners with parents to identify areas of growth and break down barriers to communication. Her greatest accomplishment is helping more than 2,000 teens and young adults find resiliency after unfortunate circumstances and assisting them in self-discovery.

She has an MBA in Social Entrepreneurship from the University of Baltimore. She is a mother of three adult children, Donte Jr., Darrius, Tania, and a wife.

Website:	www.lifeshiftgroup.com
Email:	askme@lifeshiftgroup.com
Facebook:	LIFEshift01
Twitter:	LIFEshift01

Instagram: LIFEshift_group
LinkedIn: Tanika-Craig-Speaks

I AM A VICTOR!

MELVINA L. DAVIS

GOD! I FEEL SO EMPTY!
BY MELVINA L. DAVIS

"God! I feel so empty! God! I feel so empty!" Those were the words
that I cried out in desperation to God. It is a day that will forever be
etched in my memory. It was Friday evening, March 28, 2014. The day
had started out cold but was unusually warm for the 5 pm drive home
from work. I would need to make one stop to pick up my youngest son
from the afterschool program that was 45 minutes away. Midway
through the commute, I turned off the radio because I needed silence.
In the stillness of that moment, the voice of my soul cried out loud –
God! I feel so empty! I was tired of the façade of looking successful on
the outside yet feeling unfulfilled and empty on the inside. I was
putting my energy into my marriage, my children, my career, my
home. However, somewhere along the journey, Melvina, the woman,
got lost. I felt like I was just existing. Not living life with purpose,
although it would appear that I had attained personal success. Behind
closed doors, anger and frustration were constant companions. I knew
that there was a powerful woman within waiting to manifest.

How did I get here? At times, I would think this can't be all there is to
life… navigating the ebbs and flow of a 20-year marriage, helping the
kids with homework, cleaning, cooking, and the kid's school events. I
was a proud Mom. I just felt like I was running on fumes. Being a
working mom, around the clock, and doing it well is no easy feat.
Many days when searching for myself on my to-do list, I either ran out
of day or ran out of energy. There were some years of sporadic church
attendance and church hopping to find an environment where the entire
family would participate. There were some years attempting to fit in a
side hustle. Dibbling and dabbling in entrepreneurship, i.e., network

marketing, was to be an outlet to express my gift of gab. The world of uncommon freedom had piqued my curiosity. Most of the adventures did not yield the financial rewards and stage recognition I aspired to. In fact, one of those adventures left me $11,000 in debt. Trying to do it all in my own strength, seeking and expecting external validation, and neglecting to fuel the woman within would certainly take me off the path of purpose and peace.

I felt spiritually and emotionally bankrupt. I knew I could no longer continue living this charade with such inner distress. I had come to the end of myself… or at least I had thought so. However, as the saying goes, life wasn't through with me yet! No one could have foreseen what was ahead for me within a matter of minutes of this prayer. My spiritual and emotional bank account would quickly draw down to insufficient funds.

As I continued driving down the road, I felt like I had been hit by a freight train. Boom! The driver behind me, realizing he had fallen asleep for a quick moment, had hit the gas instead of the brake. I was rear-ended and went crashing into the SUV ahead of me. The outcome was uncontrollable crying at the scene; a totaled vehicle and eight weeks off work on short term disability. There would be many doctor appointments and months of therapy to get back on the mend. In his book The Purpose Driven Life, Rick Warren quotes C.S. Lewis saying, "Pain is God's megaphone. It is God's way of arousing us from spiritual lethargy. Your problems are not punishment; they are wake-up calls…" This qualified as a wake-up call. It generated an unplanned break in my routine, causing me to slow down, to focus, to become attentive, and to place my dependence once again on Him.

A quote from Karen Salmansohn says, " It is often the deepest pain which empowers you to grow into your highest self." The brokenness I felt – spirit, soul, and body – was the catalyst plugging me back into the still small voice within my heart.

I AM A VICTOR!

I knew that God had a purpose and a plan for my life. I knew that God had more in store for me. It was and continues to be my belief that anything that He allows to happen would work out for my good.

Feeling overwhelmed and empty does not have to be the end. Pain and the feeling of being lost does not have to be a bad thing. In fact, it can signal the kickoff of the new direction or the desired transformation that is calling from within. There is a way out of a season of spiritual drought, overwhelm, and disconnection to finding fulfillment in living a more heart-centered life.

My faith, confidence, and sense of personal value have catapulted since the day of that ever-memorable prayer. I am extremely excited to have this opportunity to share the five principles that have been instrumental in helping me reconnect to the woman within, regain my confidence, and ignite my heart to create change. These principles have allowed me to experience more fulfillment and lasting confidence taking care of the true woman within. I know they will do the same for you.

5 PRINCIPLES (5PS) TO CONNECT POWERFULLY TO THE WOMAN WITHIN:

Prayer: This is what I call the God Factor. Having a daily conversation in your relationship with God. Trusting Him, being aware of His Presence, and knowing that He loves you will make all the difference in the world.

Permission: Give yourself the green light to succeed, play, rest without expecting or needing others to validate you. The validation that you need starts by saying "Yes" to yourself, thereby being unapologetically you.

Prioritize Your Selfcare – Decide to treat yourself as important. This is deciding to no longer neglect or place your needs last. On the contrary, take the time to fill your cup first and serve others from your overflow. Take the time to read, pamper yourself, or call a good girlfriend without being in a hurry.

Personal Development: This is one of my favorites. Invest in yourself. Develop the talent, hobby, or passion that fuels you. Les Brown says, "Life takes on meaning when you become motivated, set goals and charge after them in an unstoppable manner."

Partnerships: Seek out new communities and get into the company of people who are pursuing and growing in the areas you want to grow. Finding a new tribe can elevate your energy. Furthermore, do not be afraid to seek out and hire professional support for your spiritual, emotional, mental, and physical wellbeing.

Implementing these prayer strategies, permission, prioritizing self-care, personal development, and partnerships have moved my heart account from bankrupt to fulfilled. Finding purpose, making room for the woman within to courageously reveal her truest expression, and personal growth have brought so much satisfaction to my life.

Implementing these strategies will create connection, confidence, and lasting change to transform your life to experience more fulfillment, empowerment, and success!

BIO
Melvina Davis, Founder of Ignite Your Inner Power, is a motivational speaker, meeting facilitator and co-author.

Melvina helps women who are feeling overwhelmed and empty to find their fulfillment and to rekindle the fire in their hearts by tapping into the woman within.

On her own journey, while appearing to have attained external success, she experienced a season of internal discontentment and disconnection. She discovered she had lost her sense of self and reclaimed her power by implementing the plan she shares today.

I AM A VICTOR!

Melvina's Five Principle (or 5P) Plan helps women to reconnect with themselves, to increase their confidence and to ignite their hearts to create lasting change by making room for the true woman within.

Melvina serves with a spirit of excellence, a heart of integrity and desires to see women of faith excel in life and business.

Melvina L. Davis
melvinadavis4u@gmail.com
IG/FB:@melvina_davis
(484) 808-2426

LINDRIA DOCKETT

From Being to Belonging
and Back Again
By Lindria Dockett

I can count on one hand the number of times I truly wholeheartedly wished, as an adult, that I could just disappear. In remembering this day, this moment, so clearly, I can still see the 15 feet between me and a door I could easily escape to right there if I could only process what was happening. I was so taken aback by the emotion and the randomness of its timing that I simply could- not- move. The huge frog that had taken up residency in my throat prevented me from speaking; the whole scene transcended into slow motion as I realized that I had maybe 30 seconds to pull it together before a betrayal of tears would begin to flow. In a last-ditch attempt, I tried to laugh, if I could pull this off, it would buy me some time, and I prayed that a laugh would trick my brain, remove the frog, hold back the tears and by now, remove the sheer panic and redness I'm sure that was beginning to cover my face: deep breaths, Lindria. Inhale. Exhale. Lindria, THIS IS CRAZY! I silently exclaimed. What is going on with you? Get yourself together!!!

THIS moment was challenging everything I believed I was. But why? And why now??? Life was GREAT! Wasn't it? I was married to my dream guy. Mother to the perfect son! Entrepreneurship had been kind. My needs were met, and my wants knew no reasonable limitations. For as far back as I can remember, I felt great pride in how mature I was. How in control and strong and balanced I was. How independent and self-aware...There was nothing that I lacked and nothing that I needed that I couldn't obtain independently. My mother's example made sure

94

of that. She was a strong, dedicated, and fearless lady with a ridiculous work ethic. And if you could be independent to a fault - she was the poster child for it. And she is still all of those things today. She truly gave me her world. She made sure I was safe, always! Covered, always! Loved, always! It was me and her, she and I, just us two. Big Lin and Little Lin. And sharing her was not something I was particularly fond of. My favorite times were our road trips. From DC to NC and back. 3 am was the rule for our departure time.

Just us! My earliest childhood memories are on I-95S riding shotgun with my mama in a 1976 Powder Blue Chevette. I remember riding in the passenger seat on a huge yellow pillow so that I could see out the window. I vividly recall, frequently, waking as the sun was coming up to catch her driving and glancing over at me with that gaze. I didn't understand it then, but as soon as I had my first child, I knew all too well what that gaze was about. That gaze where you thank God for this precious gift, and you know nothing in life means more. The "Lord, please don't let me mess this, her, him up" prayer. Yeah, that gaze. She did that a lot. And even though it seemed weird to me at the time, it also provided a huge sense of comfort. Life is going to be Life, though, right? Do any of us really get out unscathed at all? Even with the most loving and uneventful childhood, I learned early that no matter how much of a superhero of a woman your mother is - there are some things she simply cannot give, shoes she cannot fill, questions she cannot answer, and voids she can't bury to take away. While she remains an amazing mother, and I know without question- she wanted to give me everything she didn't have growing up -- The hard reality of that is she was not a mind reader, and some things simply weren't hers to give. She couldn't give me noise in a house full of internal silence, she couldn't give me productive thoughts to replace the negative ones she never knew I was having; she couldn't dry the tears she never knew were falling, she couldn't replace the characters in my dreams with real people, and no matter how much she tried to love me through it - she couldn't make me not feel like a secret. The secret. His secret.

I AM A VICTOR!

In my childhood's quietness I had a lot of time to internalize the complexity of my being but not belonging, belonging but not belonging. Where do I belong? Knowing where you belong is a major quest to the fulfillment of life, right? And what if that answer is hidden from you - or you have been hidden from it? I can tell you what it did to me. It left me longing. Longing for love. Longing for Acceptance. Longing for Family. I filled voids with Indifference. I replaced communication with denial and avoidance. I tried to buy happiness with material possessions. I sought out surrogate friendships and relationships. I viewed my worth based on job promotions and perceived success. And then when none of that FIXED me - At 21, I planned a pregnancy with someone I only knew for a few months, and later married... and then divorced. And herein lies where all my crap came to the surface and floated... and sunk!. They say marriage is not for the faint at heart - well, it's not a good landing place when you're in complete denial about being broken either.

Growing up, I knew who my father was. Who his parents were. The city and state he lived in. What his occupation was. His work phone number. That he was married. And that I had five siblings. One - two - three - four - five siblings who knew nothing of me. The quiet times when I felt like I was dying inside trying to mask the silence, they had each other. The nights I cried myself to sleep from the imploding void of being alone in my silence, they had each other. Every holiday, birthday, and graduation that passed, they had each other. But when I dreamed of them, we were all together.

I was 18 when my father ripped the band-aid off and flew me down to meet my siblings. I was a secret no more. I was finally going from being to belonging. I was finally able to cannonball into the noisy pool of my beings, my people, my persons! It was amazing. We continued to keep in touch and see each other over the years. It has been a few years since we all have been in the same space at the same time. The very last time we all were together was nothing out of the ordinary. It was a good day. The kids were running around and playing, there was a pool game going on, dad was grilling, and everyone was laughing- in sync- while completing each other's sentences and jokes - except me. I just stood there, watching… Watching what they had together. Realizing you can't hop off of a plane after 18 years and have what they have. While I loved what I was seeing - the moment had also become very triggering for me. In remembering this day, this moment, so clearly, I can still see the 15 feet between me and a door.

I could easily escape right there if I could only process what was happening. I was so taken aback by the emotion and the randomness of its timing that I simply could - not - move. The huge frog that had taken up residency in my throat prevented me from speaking. The whole scene transcended into slow motion as I realized that I had maybe 30 seconds to pull it together before a betrayal of tears would begin to flow. In a last-ditch attempt, I tried to laugh, if I could pull this off, it would buy me some time, and I prayed that a laugh would trick my brain, remove the frog, hold back the tears, and remove the sheer panic and redness I'm sure was beginning to cover my face: deep breaths, Lindria. Inhale. Exhale.

So, I ask again. Do any of us make it out of this thing called Life unscathed? I believe not. But I also believe that is the beauty of it. To be human - just as God intended. Human enough to have a story to tell that is seasoned with experiences, checkered with mistakes, colored with victories, and painted with Faith. Knowing in life, there will be setups, setbacks, and comebacks. There can be no victory if there is no Fight.

I am a Victor over NOT BELONGING.

BIO
Lindria Dockett is a Professional Branding Photographer based in the Washington DC area. She specializes in showing Entrepreneurs, Authors, Business owners how to Visually Amplify their Brand- allowing them to Dominate in front of their Competitors! When

I AM A VICTOR!

Lindria is not assisting her clients capture savvy images to aide in building their brands - she can be found doting over her two sons (Drevian and Caleb) or enjoying a road trip to a historic location with her husband (Aaron) of 16 years.

Website: www.LindriaDockett.com
Instagram: www.Instagram.com/Lindria.Dockett
Email: VIP@LindriaDockett.com

ELIZA S. DUKES

DEEP BREATHING TRANSFORMED ME INSIDE & OUT FOREVER
BY ELIZA S. DUKES

Learning to be happy is one thing but experiencing the healing power of your breath is having the tool to shift into whatever state of being desired. I have experienced so many benefits from diaphragm breathing, which I will enjoy sharing with you.

MYSTERY ILLNESS

One morning I was washing my face and noticed a little bump under my chin. I thought it was a boil that would quickly go away. After about two weeks, the bump turned into a rather painful sizable lump, and I then arranged to see a doctor. The doctor administered test after test, and after each time the diagnosis was different. The doctor prescribed medication and insisted I take it for six months, if not, I would die. I lost confidence in the doctor and felt quite hopeless for many days until I thought back about my father's childhood experience recovering from throat cancer. Remembering my father's story helped to infuse me with such strength, it empowered me in many ways. Boldly embracing my father's healing faith, I discontinued the medication for the mysterious illness. I became willing to trust the voice of GOD within and not be another experiment. Although I believe that doctors have knowledge and wisdom in some areas. Nonetheless, more than ever, this divine spirit of guidance given by All-Knowing God was enough for me to use my faith again.

I HAD TO KEEP REPEATING MY FAVORITE SCRIPTURE

Six months later, I faced another health challenge, even greater than the mystery illness. One evening in a neighborhood I lived in, I was attacked, and the attacker cut my wrist from one side to the other while I was fighting him. I was left with no use of my wrist or fingers. After eight months of intense therapy, determination, and writing and repeating my favorite scripture, Psalms 107:20, I gained the courage with more inner strength to totally experience healing as my God-given right. I was fully persuaded as I wrote and spoke healing to myself, to trust my process, and when fear showed up, I kept declaring a full recovery over my wrist. Today I can drive and do normal things, for I have full use of my wrist and fingers well.

Through these two experiences with illness, I changed a lot. Understanding that healing is a gift and trusting God more than ever.. I love equipping others to embrace the power of healing as a new attitude of divine power.

ANOTHER PLATEAU TO CLIMB

Twelve years later, I found myself totally out of sorts, and I did not know why after all the healing experiences, here came another new challenge. I just could not shake the disturbing feelings inside myself. I had been married and divorced twice. I was a professional counselor, recording artist, prayer intercessor, and minister of music, known as the happy woman with the funny laugh. But through my pain, I learned how to hide my personal disappointments. Therefore, many nights, my heart would be so heavy, racing and waking me up in the middle of the night. And knowing what I know I said, here we go again.

I identified that my stressors and triggers were disrupting my sleep & inner peace. So, I've turned my attention to what was going on inside me, --- finding more ways to overcome the pain, anger, and disappointment had become my daily aspiration.

I AM A VICTOR!

HERE COMES MENOPAUSE

The dizziness in my head, the palpitations in my heart became the next hidden enemy. I knew I needed something fast, and I wanted it to be natural. So, after researching natural remedies for days, I was introduced to diaphragm breathing. Determined, I began to learn the power of deep breathing exercises. Before I knew it, I was constantly feeling calm, sleeping so good, my blood pressure was on point, and waking without the mental fog, was victorious for me! Yes, the symptoms of menopause began to fade with every intentional breath. The mental fog, high blood pressure, moodiness no longer was an issue, as long as I kept doing my breathing exercises. This new commitment to do the inner work, prove to me, " I Am A Victor, this changed me forever.

THE MIRACLE OF DEEP BREATHING

On this journey of self-discovery and enrichment, we must face our fears, doubts, and surprise challenges. Each challenge has spiritually empowered me to become conscious of how I treat myself. I give All-Knowing GOD so much thanks for revealing these self-therapeutic tools to become well, think well of myself and learn to be more strategic in times of uncertainty. And we are living in great uncertainty, but God has a plan to reveal to you, as well.

I am pleased to say and live as, "I Am a Victor " only because I've experienced several major healing and GOD graced me with the courage and the right. My parents made sure to share healing testimonies they personally experience. When listening to my Dad's testimonies about being healed from throat cancer, I had no idea it was a faith seed for me later—and watching my mother defy all the odds with various diseases. I could go on and on because my parents' experience built my faith and helped transform me inside when faced with my mystery illness and getting high blood pressure medications in 6 months. I've to believe and know that I know that when you are willing to grow through the healing process, apply the spiritual principles, and begin with deep breathing and meditative practices, you will become a victor continually!

Although we believe that doctors have knowledge and wisdom to practice on us. However, you can believe fir your healing begins with equipping yourself with tools to support your healing journey. With all of this, we must begin to follow the voice within, more than ever, this divine spirit of guidance of All-Knowing God is available to us all.

As we come to a close, please consider the supernatural benefits of deep breathing. Because the All-Powerful God breathed the breath of life into you, Genesis 2:7 declares. Therefore, you have access to do diaphragm breathing anytime and anywhere. This practice will reshape how to handle stress and sickness.. Here are just a few health benefits you can experience;

- The Bodies Strongest Self-Healing Tool
- Lowering Your Blood Pressure Anytime
- Naturally Strengthening the Immune System
- Increases Calmness and Clarity Easily

Through it all, my healing journey was of self-discovery and self-fulfillment, so I've overcome health challenges that truly required faith and crazy courage. I hope you ate inspired to begin using your faith, courage, and healing passages to become a Victor on purpose! I humbly give All-Knowing GOD so much thanks for opening me up to learn, self-therapeutic tools to be well, think well, and respond well in times of uncertainty and gratefully again, "I Am A Victor"

As you know, our faith is continually being tested, today especially with COVID-19. The good news is there are many tools available to you, now. Whenever you make time to connect with the Lord in quietness, you will get the instructions needed to overcome any adversity and feel His loving and comforting peace. Remember to embrace healing as a GOD-GIVEN RIGHT.

In closing, if you are a life learner like me and want all the happiness and healthiness available to you, then try the supernatural solutions GOD has made available to you. Consider making diaphragm breathing your first response to overcome the fear during this pandemic, learn to lessen anxiousness, and let go of the mental overload you may be feeling. Yes, open yourself to the supernatural realms of feeling and being well, especially in chaos. You are a gift and treasure, so be it you begin to release pressure and build your spiritual powerhouse by accepting your healing rights, too.

Let's chat soon; thanks kindly for reading my healing journey... I am a Victor, and You Are As Well!

BIO
Eliza S. Dukes, CEO of The Breathing Experience an award-winning company. Provides a mind-transforming, self-therapeutic approach to stress and dis-ease. With 20 plus years' experience in counseling and coaching, she offers mini-courses, how to utilize stress reduction methods, and proven spiritual principles that ignite a healing experience. She demonstrates, "When Breathing and Meditative Practices Become Your BFF. . Powerful Healing Energies and Happiness Will Flow With Ease" Eliza has empowered thousands of women and our traumatized youth worldwide.

Eliza is known as a Breathologist, Stress Management, and Sensational Speaker and Audio Author.

If you or someone you know feeling fearful, overwhelmed, or battling stress-related disease(s), please CALL or TEXT 302-300-1884 or visit TheBreathingExperience.com or email Ask@ElizaDukes.com for your Complimentary Clarity Session Today!

MIMI FOXWELL

When Retreat Is Not an Option
By Mimi Foxwell

"Too many of us are not living our dreams because we are living our fears."
Les Brown

Having the choice of a dream opportunity or facing a fear doesn't happen often, but I have had that experience. When the line is clearly drawn, do you step forward or retreat and run away? It was a decision I confronted in a training class.

I had finally received a long-awaited call for the new-hire training class as a flight attendant. My family was very happy for me. This would be my first job right out of school. I would be flown out of town, and my accommodations would be paid for a couple of weeks. I would receive an expense reimbursement for meals. How exciting this was for a young woman. My mom got me new clothes, a new hairdo, and I was all set for a new career. Everyone was so proud, and a friend even sent a limo to take me to the airport in style.

The training classes were intense. We were learning how to put out fires, simulating bomb threats and terrorist attacks. On this particular day, we were told to dress casually. The instructor announced there would be a change in our schedule and our training location. The change was presented as an unexpected opportunity. We would simulate our overwater evacuation not in the training room but in an actual, Olympic-sized swimming pool (where I'm told the US swim team had practiced). We were to swim to the life raft and locate the emergency equipment inside of the raft. And that would conclude our activities for the day. Easy Peasy Day.

The other trainees were squealing with delight, eager for their turn. They said, 'Oh goody, we get to be out of the classroom and swim.' I felt, WHAT! I could not swim! I was told that it was not a requirement that I know how to swim, and we were only going to "pretend" to have a mock-up in a classroom. Why did I have to be the black girl who couldn't swim? I felt like a fish out of water.

I went over to the instructor, "Excuse me, may I speak with you"? Quietly I explained my dilemma. She informed me that was fine. She has been told there were a few people with little to no swimming experience in this class. Just then, a few other non-swimmers circled around. Not to be concerned, she would meet us at the back end of the pool after she divided us into teams. She indicated that she would place me in a group with strong swimmers to help. And give me a mini-lesson. I would also have a life vest on so that everything would be fine.

As I walked to the back of the pool, my heart was pounding. I felt alone and afraid. Just looking at that deep water and imagining me in it seemed impossible. The others who gathered around included a girl who'd had a few lessons and one other person of color in the group. She was glamourous and had a lot of attitude. She was ready to slam them. How dare they schedule a black woman to get in a pool without any warning to style her hair accordingly. She was going to protest and force them to give her another option, she said with hands waving and neck rolling. She was right, I thought. They hadn't given us any consideration. I could join in with her and have a coalition.

I stood there fully dressed, yes, just as it would be if I were on board a plane. If I left now, I couldn't be guaranteed a job. I had a home-girl voice speak wisdom to me, "Girl, don't care about how you look; you do not know these people, but you know you need to get paid." I thought of the sacrifice my mother had made to buy me new clothes. I had hoped to give her some of the money back from my expense check. I thought of my grandfather, who gave me spending money, the family friend who lived near-by who came to check on me. I knew they would all say it was okay if I quit and went home.

I considered my options:

1. I could pretend to be sick, lie and possibly get another try later.
2. I could say no and leave; no one would even know I left. But I wanted this job. Would they pay to fly me back home? .
3. I could see what this mini-lesson was. After all, she couldn't let me die in a company-sponsored program.

> *"If it's important to you, you will find a way. If not, you will find an excuse."*
> Ryan Blair

My instructor gave me a quick, brief lesson. She didn't baby me or acknowledge my pain. She smiled and told me the life vest would save me. I would have a few seconds of being disoriented (six seconds, I believe she said), and the life vest would start to lift me to the surface. I could hold on to the vest, even cross my arms and count, and she would be there when I came up. She suggested I take a practice try before it was my group's turn and to call her when I was ready. She left with her clipboard and whistle.

That was it! That was to be the lesson to make me feel secure about jumping into the pool. The other two non-swimmers departed. The one who had a few lessons got in the pool and started practicing. And the other woman of color left in protest with the hope of another shot.

It was a make-or-break moment. It was not okay with me to give up. To retreat and go home was not an option. I just had to figure out a way. I chose to be open to the idea that, just maybe, I could do it. Funny how you show up for yourself when you don't even know it.

I stayed focused and calm. I decided to try. I chose not to be intimidated by the pool's size, the people watching, nor how uncomfortable and mentally challenging this was. I thought of what the instructor said that I'd be disoriented for a few seconds. Seconds was not going to send me home. I was a victor at that point. Bring it on; I wasn't looking for the exit but the other side of completed. I had bought into there being a way, a process to success.

I focused on a way to let my body be submerged and not panic. I released my body from the edge of safety and went in! Stepping into danger isn't easy, but I had equipment. I had that life vest, faith, and a process.

Oh man, a few seconds never seemed so long. Disoriented is another way to say you're going to freak out. Trying not to panic took a lot of belief. But I did it. I joined the team of good swimmers the instructor placed me in. I pushed my body the best I could through the water and could barely get my legs around the double chambers of the 40+ person raft.

As I changed out of my wet clothes, back in my room, my whole body was exhausted. My mind was on overload. I thought I had no cheerleader today. No one knew how brave I'd been or cared how difficult it was. It made me realize there will be battles and victories you'll have, and no one will even know your fight.

 I want to leave you with some tips I learned along the way when confronted with an obstacle.

1. Allow yourself to believe in possibilities.
2. Stay calm so you can center yourself and listen to the knowing voice that will come.

3. Reach into yourself and pull it out. We focus on what's hard instead of what we have.
4. Find your own process that makes sense to you and run with it.

BIO

Mimi Foxwell is a certified mediator and restorative justice facilitator who is on a soulful mission to help others have peace in their lives. As a coach and consultant, she brings a creative approach for women to uncover their true leadership potential and legacy.

Mimi's BA in Psychology from Clark Atlanta University was only the start for her on the study of human behavior that includes a certification in positive psychology and social/emotional learning.

As the founder of Conflict 2 Calm, she focuses on increasing emotional wellness.

When not speaking or coaching on emotional intelligence Mimi can be found pursuing her passion for crafting, increasing her wine expertise, and spending time with her family.

To connect with Mimi
Conflict2Calm.com
IG @sisterintheroom

DR. JONAS GADSON

FACING YOUR FUTURE WITH A NEW FOCUS!
BY DR. JONAS GADSON, DTM - KNOWN AS "MR. ENTHUSIASTIC!"

There are three kinds of people…Those who make things happen, those who watch things happen, and those who wonder, "What happened?" I am a person who makes positive things happen, and I believe that you are too! Bonus from Jonas, "Your future is so bright that you are going to need to wear sunglasses!" "Don't Focus On What You Have Lost! Focus On What You Have Left! Because What You Have Left Is Enough To Get the Job Done!" "You Are Next In Line For A Blessing! Don't Get Out of Line, Don't Detour, and Don't Let Anyone Cut In Front of You! It's Full Steam Ahead! Because whatever you focus on the longest will become the strongest!" This chapter will show you that you can face your future with a new focus! Because I have learned that "the best way to predict the future is to create it!" This is your time, and this is your turn! Congratulations on your wise decision to invest in the most important person on the planet, you! Bonus from Jonas, "A chapter a day keeps mediocrity away and welcomes greatness in to stay!" Welcome in greatness! In this chapter, we will deal with the 5 V's: Vision is where you are going. Value is your foundation. Valley is what you must grow through. Voice: You deserve to be heard. And Victor is celebrating the things that you have overcome!

Vision is what you can be; eyesight is what you can see. Some people have 20/20 eyesight but no vision. What do you see for your future? Bonus from Jonas, "What you see is what you will be! And if you want to be more, you have to first see more!"

My favorite book says that "without vision, the people perish. But with vision, the people will flourish." "Write the vision, make it plain, then run with it!" "If You Think it; Ink it!" Once your vision is clear, you must take positive action to bring it to reality.

A young reporter looking to make a name for himself ran up to Ms. Helen Keller. He said to her, "Life must have been very difficult for you. Being blind and not able to see." Ms. Helen Keller answered him and said, "Worse than being blind is having sight but no vision."

BONUS FROM JONAS

"When your vision is clear, the results will appear!"

I have learned that the biggest room in the whole wide world is room for improvement! You can always Better your Best! In this decade, you must implement the two w's: work and worth. I like what the great orator Frederick Douglas said, "You might not get everything that you work for, but you must work for everything you get!" Whitney Young said, "It is better to be prepared for an opportunity and not have one than to have an opportunity and not be prepared!" When we don't take the time to prepare, then we will spend our life in repair! When you work on yourself and know that you are worth it, you will do the work!

BONUS FROM JONAS

"When your value is clear, your decision is easy!"

Value is what you believe in strongly. It is the foundation that all of your principles, beliefs, and integrity are built upon. It is your anchor, your foundational block, your guiding light, your compass. It is what helps you to navigate through the storms of life. It is non-negotiable! When you have value, your word is your bond. "What you say and what others see is working together in harmony!" The four foundational blocks of value in my coaching business are Education, Inspiration, Transformation, and Motivation! I challenge you to define your value because you are doomed to follow someone else's if you don't.

Valley. Sometimes in life, we find ourselves in the valley, and our goal is to get through it as fast as we can! However, it is better to grow through the valley. Then when we arrive on the other side, we are better for it! If we didn't learn the lesson when we were in the valley, we will end up repeating the course! If you are in the valley in your life now, here is how you get out:

Don't Nurse it! Don't give it the nutrients and vitamins for it to grow. It is impossible to feed yourself negative thoughts and live a positive life.

Don't Curse it! You are bitter and spewing negativity on yourself and on others.

Don't Rehearse It! I ask, How long ago did this happen? 20 years ago!? I expected that you would say 20 minutes ago! You died so that this negativity can live?! Let it go so you can grow!

BONUS FROM JONAS
"Reverse It!"

You start the process to become a new you by implementing new skills in your life. They are lessons that you have learned, and now you are making better decisions.

BONUS FROM JONAS
"You cannot change your past, but you can change your path!"

Voice. You deserve to be heard! We need to hear your voice telling your story!

My Story Of Overcoming The Tumor In My Stomach! I was born in 1953 in Beaufort, South Carolina, at Beaufort Memorial Hospital; I was a healthy baby. And I was raised on St. Helena Island, SC, on a plantation. But when I was a little boy of four years old, I became very sickly, and my stomach was protruding out as if I were nine months pregnant! My mother didn't know what was wrong. I was the sickest child out of all of her eleven children. And I got worse! Then my mother rushed me to Roper Hospital in Charleston, SC. At four years old, I had to undergo major surgery; my life was at stake!

I had a tumor in my stomach; that was why my stomach was protruding out as if I were nine months pregnant. The doctors told my mother that they had operated on eight other babies who had the same condition I had, and all eight of the other babies died and that I was going to be number nine! And they operated on me, not expecting me to live.

I remember coming out of surgery, heavily sedated and in pain, stitches all in my stomach. Before I could recover, the doctors discovered that I had a massive infection! And I had to have a second operation immediately! When the doctors went back into my right side to clean up the horrible infection, they realized that it had spread to my right kidney, and they took that kidney out without telling my mother and without telling me. I now had two operations, one on my stomach and the second on my right side near my ribs and my back! These two surgeries resulted in a very long journey on the road of recovery for me. I had gone into the hospital with a protruding stomach and came out with one kidney and with two deep wounds and a limp that should have stayed with me for life. But it didn't! I am an overcomer! The doctors had given me a diagnosis that I would die, but God gave me the final prognosis, that I would live!"

BONUS FROM JONAS

"Don't let anyone bury you until after you are dead.

I AM A VICTOR!

You are bigger than that. You are better than that! And the best is still in you! Allow that Best to Bud, to Bloom, and to Blossom Into A Bright and Beautiful Future!"

I am a Victor! The things that I overcame not only happened to me, but they also happened for me. By showing you my story, it has not only strengthened me, but it has helped hundreds of thousands of others. When you implement the 5 V's into your life immediately, then you too will be a victor!

Now when you show and tell your story, you design your own future and face it with a new focus! You are on your way to the top and cannot be stopped! The sky is not your limit; your belief is.

BONUS FROM JONAS

"If you cheat yourself in your preparation,
it will show up in your presentation."

Now you know that "the best way to predict your future is to create it!" Bonus from Jonas, "Read this chapter the first time for information. Then read it a second time to start your transformation!" Congratulations! On investing in the Most Important Person on the Planet, You!

You must learn how to Master Your Message! Know yourself, know your subject and know your specific audience. As an Expert Communication Coach, I can teach you how to show your story and not just tell it!

"Since Greatness Is Possible Excellence Is Not Enough!
Go For Greatness!"

Get Your FREE gift and learn more about how to Master Your Message! "How To Give A Powerful Presentation!" Go to: www.jonasbonus.com/freegift

BIO

Dr. Jonas Gadson, DTM, known as "Mr. Enthusiastic!" is an International Motivational Speaker, Trainer, Author, Radio Personality and Expert Communication Coach. He worked 30 years for two Fortune 500 companies, Xerox Corporation and Eastman Kodak Company. At Eastman Kodak Company he trained over 8,000 employees from 69 countries and earned the Trainer of the Year Award. In 2020, he was inducted into the Marquis Who's Who In America, he spoke at the Wonder Women Tech Virtual Summit in London, England, the Worldwide Multicultural Summit, and the Black Speakers Network. He is a Distinguished Toastmaster, DTM, a graduate of Dale Carnegie and has a Doctorate Degree in Theology. He was inducted into the Beaufort High School Alumni Hall of Fame for distinguishing himself in profession, leadership, and service! He has been featured in Speakers Magazine, Pink Magazine and Beaufort Lifestyle Magazine!

Dr. Jonas Gadson, DTM – jg@jonasbonus.com (585) 703-9547 www.jonasbonus.com

I AM A VICTOR!

MIJIZA A. GREEN

PRESSED, PREPPED & PUSHED
INTO MY PURPOSE
BY MIJIZA A. GREEN

July 11, 1993, Brooklyn NY

I lay in a hospital bed about to give birth to a baby boy. I am in so much pain, but I refuse to let anyone know. It has been three days of labor; the contractions are 2 minutes apart. My mother sits beside me, wishing she could rewind the hands of time. I am wondering how we got here. In the background, I hear screaming and praying from other women who are in labor.

The doctor checks my cervix; he says, "she has not dilated past 8 centimeters; if this does not change soon, we will have to take the baby by an emergency C-section". As I listen along, I wonder what a C-section is, thinking, no! They cannot take my baby. He is mine; I know I messed up, but mom, you said we would be okay. I lay there in complete fear that they will take my baby.

As I lay in the bed, I hear the doctors talking about me. They are saying she is so young, where is the father? Should we call child protective services? My mom is not clear what to do as she awaits my father. I wanted my dad. I wanted him to take the pain away; I wanted him to make it all better. This time I was alone. No one could make it better. I ask myself; how did I get here? What did I get myself into? I am supposed to be starting high school in 2 months. I am supposed to be playing outside on my way to the pool, but for now, I will be prepping to give birth at the age of 13. My birthday is in 2 weeks;

happy birthday to me because this was the last day of being a kid. The doctor preps me, gives me an epidural, and says I am sorry, we must do this, but your body is not ready for a baby to come out the normal way. I leave my mom behind as I am wheeled off into the surgery room. I am not sure what is going on or if I will make it out alive, but I did learn how to pray one time at church, so I will try that. I prayed and told God I was sorry for being such an embarrassment to my family; I was sorry for trying to be grown and doing the horizontal poker (that is what I called sex). I told him I promised I would be on my best behavior and be the best I can be if I make it. They cut me; I should say that doctor scarred me in so many ways for the rest of my life. Through his words, his attitude, and the fact that he cut my stomach in such a way, I began to believe it was my punishment for having a baby. I started to believe that this cut on my stomach would be my constant reminder of my shame of having a baby at 13.

After several suicide attempts, including cutting my wrist, drinking liquor, smoking weed to make it go away, nothing worked. I went skiing on my 8th-grade senior trip and went down the slope, purposely falling each time to try to kill myself or get rid of this baby, that did not work. I attempted an abortion twice. It seemed like it worked for others in my neighborhood, but it did not work for me. My parents found out through a phone call home after several rumors floated around my school, the guidance counselor called me to confirm the rumors, and I told her everything; it felt like a weight lifted. Finally, I can stop holding my stomach in; finally, someone noticed me, finally, someone would help. The phone call led to me telling my mom and led to a doctor's appointment where we were told that the only way to abort the baby was to go to Canada because by the time my parents found out, it was the month of May, and I was already almost seven months pregnant. Could you imagine not being noticed at 13 years old? I was a straight-A student, gaining weight, isolating myself, but no one noticed but my middle sister. She tried her best to help in many ways. She cut school to take me to the doctor and pretend to be my guardian; she let me wear her clothes to disguise my stomach. She told me she would be there for me no matter what, and she was.

121

I AM A VICTOR!

After two months of bed rest from May to July, I finally gave birth to a healthy 7lbs 11 oz baby boy on the seventh month and 11th day of the year. Some may say he was a lucky baby; I have grown to understand that he was a blessing. That 13-year-old girl turned 14 years old two weeks later made a vow to herself. She promised to learn to be the best mother she could; she promised to finish high school; she promised to make her parents proud of her even if she spent a lifetime doing it. She promised never to give up no matter how hard life got. Life was hard for her when others were partying, and being a teen, she came home to study and take care of her child. When others were having boy problems, she was hoping her 15-year-old child's father would come home from jail.

My high school years were not easy; I had experienced so many things a teen should never have to. I went through an identity crisis, trying to figure out who I was and where I was going—always fighting to find my way and where I fit in. I was always different; I was darker than my other family members, I was bigger than my peers, and I had already learned how to keep secrets. I hid the fact that a family member molested me, and I hid a pregnancy for seven months. No one knew I had experienced domestic violence or understood the pain I felt when my sons' father was murdered, and finally, in my senior year, a trip to a psychiatric center for a few months. I had experienced all this in only a few years, and I was still a teen. I knew I was different; how could I have survived this and still be in my sane mind? That is when I knew it had to be that church visit when I was younger. I gave my life to Jesus but never knew what it meant. He had to have been with me through all of this. I went to college, moved to Maryland for a better life for my son and me, and started a new life. I had another son ten years later, got married, had another baby boy, obtained a business degree, am currently working on a psychology degree, started a youth program, started a business, wrote a book, and so much more.

You see, I am a Victor, that underdog, the one that when the world counted out, God counted me in. When I realized that I had spent a lifetime proving to the world that I was worth it, that I was qualified, that I was deserving to do the things I was doing, I stopped being the underdog and became the frontwoman. I did not need to hide anymore. I knew what my purpose was; it was to change the world, it was to mentor girls, it was to understand that my story is about me but not for me as Dr. Cheryl Wood says. All the things I had experienced in life were for a reason, for a purpose, and I was okay with it and would not change a thing. My experiences shaped and molded me into the woman I am today, and it is time to tell the world.

I want you to take this with you in your heart and use my techniques to help release the pain, help you be the best version of yourself, accept the cup that was given to you, and let God do the rest. No more shame, no more tears. It is time to be the new you. Never give up; use your pain to motivate you, stop holding on to the past and share your story.

You can achieve these by using the acronym S.E.L.F.:

> **STOP** crying, being angry, depression and anxiety
>
> **EVALUATE** your life (dig deep)
>
> **LISTEN** to the voice, dreams, and goals in your head. (You are not crazy)
>
> Lastly, **FORGIVE** yourself; it is not your fault, and forgive those who hurt you.

I am here to help you start your journey to healing. For more information about S.E.L.F techniques in life, leadership, and love, contact me. IT'S YOUR TIME! Let it go; you are no longer the underdog; YOU ARE A VICTOR!

BIO
Mijiza Green is the Owner of Planting Seeds Community Outreach, where she is a youth program consultant and has helped develop customized youth programs such as Treasured Jewels Mentor Program,

I AM A VICTOR!

Young Men Empowered and GRACE Empowerment that has Inspired, Educated, and Impacted many lives in the DMV and surrounding areas.

Mijiza has worked for reputable community organizations including, The EPICENTER, Boys and Girls Club, YMCA, and HCPS, among others. Mijiza is an impactful speaker, mentor, author, and coach who has dedicated her life to helping youth and young adults become leaders by building character, confidence, and courage through her S.E.L.F techniques. Sacrifice, Empathize, Learn and Focus which are important characteristics in leadership and life.

Mijiza is a married to Nathanal Green, mother of 4 and nana to 2 grandchildren all while being employed and pursuing a second degree at Morgan State University.

TONYA Y. GRIFFIN

Suffering in Silence: F**k Chronic Illness
By Tonya Y. Griffin

"Lord, I need you, I have not and will not lose faith in you, but I feel that I'm losing my way and drowning in a sea of pain and disease. I know I'm in a dark place right now, but I beg you, Father God, please take my hand and anchor me through these rough waters. I need you..." That was the silent prayer I whispered to myself while lying in the Emergency Room due to chronic illness. Over the past few years, I've been to the hospital dozens of times. Each time leaving with a sense of humility, exhaustion, and the feeling of being unheard or misunderstood. I've been suffering in silence with undiagnosed autoinflammatory/autoimmune diseases for years. Several years before this ER visit, I was diagnosed with a non-curable autoinflammatory skin disease called Hidradenitis Suppurativa (HS), which causes painful, inflamed, and infected boils throughout the body. A few short months before lying in the Emergency Room, I was diagnosed with Rheumatoid Arthritis and Hypothyroidism.

Each autoimmune/autoinflammatory flare is different from the next, becoming more intense, longer-lasting, and more debilitating. This flare-up, however, was like no other flare that I've experienced. I suffered from extreme body pain, headaches, loss of appetite, loss of sleep, extreme exhaustion, and severe brain fog. The constant oozing drainage from my HS nodules became infected, swollen, and painful to touch, and my joints were all painfully swollen. This experience was one that I knew needed immediate medical attention, which is how I landed in the ER once again. At this point, the stabbing pain that

126

radiated from my joints and through the wound site infection was growing more and more intense. I was desperate for relief and in need of a miracle. One that would take away the excruciating pain.

My sister quietly pulled up a chair next to my bed. From the corner of my eye, I was able to take a quick glimpse at the look of fear on her face. I felt vibrations of her hand trembling on her knee from the bed. As a way to break the silence and redirect our thoughts towards something more positive, she quickly scrolled her phone playlist to find Tamela Mann's song "Take Me to the King," which later became my daily anthem during my healing and recovery journey. The beautiful but powerful melody echoed throughout the small hospital room, almost pulsating from the walls into my head, breaking the flow of negative thoughts filling my mind throughout my wait. The temporary feelings of joy quickly passed once the door began to slide open. As the drifty smell of antiseptic from the hallway filled the air, the smell immediately triggered involuntary thoughts and memories of my past four hospital stays and three emergency surgeries that had taken place less than nine months before this visit. At that moment, I knew that I had to mentally prepare for whatever the outcome would be.

As the nurse entered the room, I overheard the doctor behind her say they would keep me for overnight observation. My heart sank. Not to my surprise, what was supposed to have been one night of observation turned into two intense weeks of round the clock antibiotics, blood draws, scans, and tests. Most of the time was a blur, but I recall feeling miserable, broken, and helpless, knowing my body was rapidly deteriorating from sepsis as time passed. Day after day, I laid limp in the hospital room, desperate for signs of improvement while praying that God could hear my pleas for help. On day seven, God answered my cries in the form of a doctor that came to observe my condition daily. As always, the doctor pulled his usual chair to the foot of my bed to discuss my daily treatment plan. During his routine discussion, he stopped, paused, and said:

I AM A VICTOR!

"Ms. Griffin, I know you love your family, and you want to get out of here to be with them, but after you leave, you need to understand that based on your personal and professional situation, your healing may be delayed due to your stress. Stress can kill people, and if you let it, it can and will kill you... please don't give up." I heard him loud and clear, but my mind seemed only to be fixated on the fact that I would possibly be taken away from my family. From that day forward, I knew that tremendous change would have to take place from within myself to heal and be free from the burdens of these illnesses, which included limiting my personal and professional stressors if I wanted to survive. After two weeks in the hospital, I was strong enough to finally be discharged home with another surgery scheduled soon after my discharge.

A month later, still weak and recovering from my previous hospital stay, my much-needed surgery left me disabled and unable to care for myself properly. Over the next year, my healing and recovery journey consisted of being bedridden for six months, regaining my mobility and strength in both arms and legs, 24-hour care and assistance from my family for everything from eating, drinking, going to the restroom to cleaning my body. I also required assistance from a home health nurse three days a week. Never in a million years would I have thought that I would be in a situation where walking, using the restroom, combing my hair, or even opening bottled water would be a struggle that required me to request assistance.

As the recovery process prolonged, so did the reality that I could not continue working at my place of employment, where I had diligently devoted more than 20 years. As days went on, it was prevalent that my body could not handle the daily stressors of my job, and resignation or medical retirement was my only alternative. After weighing my options, I chose to medically retire at 41. This decision was heartbreaking and a pivotal turning point forcing me to re-evaluate what was most important within my life. I had to accept and embrace my new role of being a stay-at-home mom while recovering from an illness and surgery. The transition was not natural for me, but over time I began to enjoy my new role and was ready and devoted to being 100% present for my household.

Surviving the physical, mental, and financial pitfalls and challenges of chronic illness have allowed me the opportunity to strengthen my faith and relationship with God and his divine powers of healing. God placed on my heart the gift of empathy and compassion to help others through chronic illness. I now dedicate my life to advocating, educating, empowering, and encouraging others through their life, wellness, and career transition journey. I have also become an advocate for myself by refusing to be seen by any medical team that does not fully support my healing.

Instead of feeling discouraged or depressed when my body is exhausted or weak or pushing through the pain, I now listen to the little messages my body sends me. If I'm feeling weak, I rest. If I'm stressed, I meditate. If I need help, I ask instead of silently suffering in the shadows. I have no problem with saying F*CK chronic illness and press forward with my day. It took me over a year to find my path towards healing. Readjusting my lifestyle to live by what I call my "7 rules" to optimize and maintain my health has become my new sense of normal. These seven rules have helped me prioritize self-care in my daily routine to live the quality of life I choose to live.

My 7 rules of optimal health are:
1. Practice gratitude and mindfulness.
2. Increase nutrition through whole foods, supplements, and herbal remedies.
3. Find a team of supportive individuals that will help when needed.
4. Seek out alternative pain management therapies.
5. Practice daily self-care.
6. Eliminate as much exposure to toxins, negative stress.
7. Find spiritual comfort.

I AM A VICTOR!

Finding your own path to healing by keeping your faith, being positive, and staying consistent is imperative. While recovering, I came across a bible verse. 2 Corinthians 1:8-10:

"We were crushed and overwhelmed beyond our ability to endure, and we thought we would never live through it. In fact, we expected to die. But as a result, we stopped relying on ourselves and learned to rely only on God, who raises the dead."

No matter how dark your path may be or how far we lose our way, we are reminded how precious and unique our lives are every day. We were made to be perfectly imperfect!! Stop relying on ourselves to walk this road alone but trust in God or your higher power to take those steps with you. Your true strength and courage will fall between the air underneath your feet and the road that God has paved towards your journey.

BIO

Tonya Griffin is the owner of Tonya Griffin Coaching and Wellness, LLC. She is an author, Functional Medicine Practitioner, Certified Holistic Life, Wellness and Career Coach, Certified Herbalist, and Certified Womb Care Facilitator, Tonya provides coaching and wellness support and services for women recovering from autoimmune/autoinflammatory disease, injuries, illness, or transitioning from job loss due to illness or injury.

She currently uses her platform to empower, encourage, and educate women through their natural healing, recovery, and self-care journey. A native of Portland, Oregon, Tonya currently resides in Hoover, Alabama with her partner Ronald, five beautiful children and younger sister.

You can learn more about Tonya, book a service, purchase classes, products, or resources, visit:
Website: https://tonyagriffincoaching.com
Email: Tonya@tonyagriffincoaching.com

Follow Tonya on social media:

FB: Tonya Griffin Coaching and Wellness
https://www.facebook.com/tonya.griffin.142687,
YouTube Channel:
https://www.youtube.com/channel/UCghmulgUS8ptNB8lvYU
QYtg

I AM A VICTOR!

DUANIA HALL

I Am Not Okay!
By Duania Hall

Suicide - the act or instance of taking one's own life voluntarily and intentionally.

I never wanted to talk about my experience with suicide. It's one of those taboo things that nobody really wants to be associated with. Most people don't even want to admit that they have ever had suicidal thoughts. And nobody wants to confess that they tried to kill themselves... but I did.

When I was in junior high school, my class went on a trip to the mountains. It was a beautiful summer day. There were big, tall trees, squirrels on the hunt, rustic cabins, hiking trails, and the sound of a nearby stream. There was also an area where boys played basketball and girls were perfecting their Double Dutch moves and lip gloss application. My best friend let me borrow her white shorts to match her and the other girls in our cabin.

While playing outside, Aunt Flow came. I rushed to the bathroom, looking for something to make a pad from but was unlucky. Blood started flowing fast & heavy, and now the shorts were turning shades of red! I didn't want my classmates to see blood all over me, so I went outside to find an adult. When I didn't find help, I determined that the best thing to do was wash the shorts.

My mother often stressed never putting just one thing in the washer, so I took the hidden route back to the cabin and grabbed some other clothes. I really didn't know how to wash, so I mixed all the clothes together. Now, the washing machine was a perfect picture for a Skittles commercial as blues, greens, and reds were running around in the washer like a track star! The white shorts now mimicked a bad version of a tie-dye shirt. My friend's shorts were ruined! I panicked, and when my best friend found out what happened, she yelled and commenced to calling me all the names I wasn't born with! Then she ended our years of friendship. I was devastated.

Aside from losing my best friend, I was struggling at home. My parents' love language shifted to insulting each other or arguing about everything, and my older sister seemed irritated by my existence. And if that wasn't enough, my boyfriend broke up with me because I wasn't ready to have sex. To make matters worse, I was having trouble focusing on schoolwork, and I, the A student, fell off the honor roll. Now, I had disappointed both my parents and teachers. In my adolescent mind, I was failing at everything!

For days I felt horrible and couldn't sleep. I made up a story about feeling sick so that I could stay home from school. My emotions were in a tug-o-war, and I was surrounded by replays of everything I was going through. It felt as if a volcano was erupting inside my heart and head. I was unhappy. I felt discarded and stupid! I didn't know what to do, and it hurt. The pain of my problems was greater than anything I had felt before. I JUST WANTED IT TO STOP.

There were prescription medications in the bathroom cabinet. I knew if I took a lot of them, it could help me go to sleep permanently. I grabbed three bottles of random pills, some water and settled in on the couch in the den. Then while watching television, I kept swallowing pills until I felt drowsy.

The next thing I heard was a voice shouting in the distance, "Don't let her sit down; I don't care if she is tired; you have to keep her moving." Someone else was walking me back and forth in rounds. I remember

135

complaining that I wanted to go to sleep, and I kept falling. They grabbed me and said, "come on, you gotta stay up." After being walked up and down a familiar path, I was given some concoction and started vomiting everywhere!

I was blessed that someone found me in time and knew how to get me to throw up the pills. I didn't have to go to a hospital and have my stomach pumped so this incident could be concealed. But I wish that cultural norms had risen above the need for secrecy. And I wish it was socially acceptable for me to say, "I AM NOT OKAY," and for my parents to say, "I don't know how to help my child get through this." But at that time, things weren't like that. There's a popular saying, "what happens in Vegas stays in Vegas." It's the same rule in some households. Children are told, "what happens in this house stays in this house." This was the case in my house growing up; while I value privacy, the "Vegas" mentality often keeps people from getting the help they need.

Another reason people don't reveal having suicidal thoughts is that it conflicts with the image they are expected to uphold. People also don't disclose suicidal thoughts because others automatically look at them as if they are crazy. Suicide is the 2nd leading cause of death for people ages 10-34. Are they crazy? NO! Some things we experience in life are hard! People should be able to say I am having suicidal thoughts, I am depressed, or I am not okay. We should not respond with judgment or use their pain for gossip. We need to love them more, listen to them more, pray for and with them more, and show up for them more. How we handle each other matters and can be the difference in whether someone chooses to live and talk about their problems or die to escape the problems they believed they didn't have permission to share.

I don't believe my family had the tools to know how to help me the way that I needed, and I didn't know what to ask for. Hindsight has taught me that I needed them to get help for me. I think therapy would have been a great way to identify what led to me making what could have been a devastating and permanent decision. God saw the gap my family had in dealing with my suicide attempt and the gap I had with processing my feelings as an adolescent. He filled the gaps by placing certain people in my life. Those people helped me realize that God valued me and that I could make it through anything with God. Despite other traumatic experiences I've had, suicide is no longer an option.

As a result of healing, I've enjoyed the harvest of victory over suicide for over 30 years! My harvest includes having two amazing children with whom I have broken the cycle of the "Vegas" mentality household. I've also been blessed to help many people who trusted me with their moments of having suicidal thoughts or sharing how their loved one attempted suicide. I'm so grateful God chose me to be of service in this way because we all need somebody to support us and listen, without judgment, when we share the most vulnerable parts of ourselves. And we all need someone to remind us that our life matters.

Around 800,000 people commit suicide every year, and there are approximately 25 times more suicide attempts. There are many things I didn't understand when I attempted suicide, but what I know for sure is that it takes a village to help hurting people heal. Here are some preventative strategies on how to help people who may be struggling with suicidal thoughts.

Tips:
1. **Have a regular check-in with your loved ones.** This goes beyond "How was your day" or "What's wrong with you?" Let them know you 'see' them and care about their well-being.
2. **Communicate effectively.** Ask straight questions without making them feel judged. Also, listen with the intent to understand. If someone confides in you, allow them to talk freely and without interruption. It's important to show you care and want to support them.
3. **Be intentional about getting to know the youth you're around.** This includes observing their behavior, noticing

changes in behavior, and determining a bad mood versus a shift in their character's dynamic.

4. **Use Talking Tools.** Sometimes parents and teachers need help communicating with children, especially when they are in that 'one-word phase.' A good source for having meaningful conversations is Teen Talk in a Jar and Let's Talk Conversation Cards for Teens.

Resources:

- Visit https://www.suicideispreventable.org/to learn more about depression, anxiety, suicide, and prevention.
- Call the National Suicide Lifeline 1800-273-8255
- https://borislhensonfoundation.org
- https://mindfulschools.org (Talking Tools)

Lastly, I am a victor because I found purpose in my pain and because I choose life every day...for me, for my children, and for every hurting person I can inspire. I pray that from this day forward, you get up each day and choose to live!

BIO

Duania Hall is a motivational speaker, best-selling author, and empowerment coach whose mission is to inspire women to begin again after trauma, maximizing their lives through self-care. A social work background and surviving multiple traumas has guided her in helping others navigate through their own traumatic experiences. Duania has spent the last 15 years helping survivors of domestic violence rebuild their lives and connect with resources. She is passionate about increasing awareness of domestic violence, suicide prevention, and other trauma while educating organizations on how to better serve survivors. In her spare time, she creates and facilitates empowerment workshops designed to help survivors communicate their needs and reclaim their power. You can follow Duania or inquire about hiring her for your next event on the following platforms:

Instagram: dh_motivating4life
Facebook: DKHall
Email: dkhallfirst@gmail.com

I AM A VICTOR!

PASTOR PAULETTE HARPER

THE FINAL FOUR WORDS
BY PASTOR PAULETTE HARPER

"And David enquired at the Lord, saying, 'Shall I pursue after this troop? shall I overtake them?' And he answered him, 'Pursue: for thou shalt surely overtake them, and without fail recover all.'"
1 Samuel 30:8 KJV

Have you ever felt stuck? Have you ever been in a place where it felt as though life paused or it stood still? Have you ever felt paralyzed or totally numb when you receive some news you didn't want to hear?

I've been there. I know that space personally. I was about to embark on a new journey I was not prepared for, nor did I embrace.

My life changed forever when I heard these words:

I. Want. A Divorce.

As co-pastor and First Lady, I prayed and trusted divorce wouldn't be my reality. I remember walking into our bedroom closet, and all of his clothes were gone.

That's the moment time stood still. I fell to the ground, curled up like a baby, and cried uncontrollably. I was about to become a divorced preacher who was called to inspire others with hope, yet at that very moment, I was left feeling as if I had no hope at all.

We married in our early twenties. By forty, I was divorced. I had invested everything into him, our marriage, the ministry, and our children. I had nothing left to give. I was empty, except for the gamut of emotions I was now experiencing from hopelessness, severe depression, feelings of fear, loneliness, shame, and even thoughts of suicide.

"Go ahead, Paulette. Jump off the bridge. Take those pills, and it will be all over. Nobody cares about you, anyway." At forty, I didn't have the will to live because everything I'd built was in him. So, at forty, I was alone. At forty, I was suicidal. At forty, I had no hope. At forty, I was abandoned.

At forty, I was dealing with emotional trauma and asking God, "Where are You?"

According to the Center for Integrated Health Solutions, in the United States 61% of men and 51% of women report exposure to at least one lifetime traumatic event.

I was now part of those stats. Trauma doesn't take a long time to have an impact on your life. In a matter of moments, those four words and his absence had traumatized me.

I had been hurt before, but this was different. This hurt was deep, deep within the core of who I was. I had no idea what I was about to face, nor was I prepared for it.

This man who I had known since I was fourteen walked out of my life, never to return. I didn't know how to get past the rejection, the feelings of abandonment, the hurt, the shame, the fear, and the effects of the divorce. How could I get past the things he said, his actions, or even the fact he had quickly moved on with his life with someone else? I wish I could say I immediately recovered, but I

143

can't. The days following, I found myself going deeper and deeper into depression and despair. All my years of being taught spiritual warfare and even standing in the gap for others, I couldn't muster enough energy to fight for myself, let alone pray. I was under attack emotionally, spiritually, and physically. The spiritual battle was the war going on in my mind and the voices of defeat that rang loud and clear. Physically, I was battling with migraine headaches as I have never experienced before. Those migraines greeted me in the mornings and remained with me for the duration of the divorce proceedings. No pill I tried relieved me of the anguish, no matter how many I swallowed or the brand I took. I was on a downhill spiral, and all I wanted was the pain to leave, but the migraines were a constant reminder of what was going on internally. It was more debilitating than what was happening externally.

After being married for twenty-three years and experiencing one of the darkest moments in my life, I had to ask myself, "How did you get here, and how will you get out of this hell hole?" How could I find myself even when I didn't want to be found? Even in the darkest of moments of life, God was there all the time. He gave me glimpses of hope when, out of nowhere, two sisters from the past crossed my path. One was a phone call from another pastor's wife whom I hadn't seen or heard from in years, and the other sister and I greeted each other in the bathroom of a church I was attending. Time and divine intervention had kissed, and it was in those moments I knew His hand was still on my life, and He indeed had more for me to do. These two sisters took me under their wings, prayed for me, spoke the Word over my life, and helped me to see there was another chapter in my life to write. The process of restoration began, but what did that look like? It had to begin in my mind and the words I was using and confessing over my life. It started with changing my mindset, who I was, and who I wanted to become. I refuse to believe that God allowed me to go through in vain. I had to believe the pain and heartbreak I was experiencing had a purpose, and I was determined to find out what it was. With that, it required me to take drastic steps to ensure I would heal, recover all, and be positioned to move ahead without fear, doubt, or worry.

Here's what I did that helped me claim the victory. Maybe you find yourself in the same predicament as I was and need help along the journey. What worked for me can also work for you. Apply it to your life, and watch God restore your life just as He's done mine. One of the things I felt we could have done to help our marriage was counseling, but he refused to join me. So, I went alone. My focus wasn't to save my marriage— that was over. My focus was on saving myself. I believe it is important to have sound counsel and friends we can confide in during these hard times. I needed to forgive myself and others. Sometimes it was hard to do, but my future depended on it. I had to forgive the man who caused me the most hurt. Forgive the man who forever changed my life and the lives of our children. I had to forgive him for the words he spoke into my spirit, and I had to forgive myself for allowing those words and the lies from the enemy that trapped me into a belief system that almost killed me. I used daily affirmations from the Bible and quotes I found online. I printed them out and placed them all over my house, including the mirrors in my bathroom and on my refrigerator. They were my daily reminders to uplift and encourage myself while I walked through the storm. As God helped me heal, I learned my voice needed to be heard, and my story had the power to change lives.

With newfound resolve and hope, I forged ahead, knowing that God was with me every step of the way. Women ask me how I overcame those challenges? I was committed to doing the transformational work requiring me to go deep within myself and receive a clearer direction from God. With that... I found my purpose for the pain. The purpose for the divorce. It was for countless other women who had stories just like mine. Over time, my confidence began to rise because I finally could see a new beginning. And it started with me. I began to reinvent myself. I reinvented who I was as a child of the

I AM A VICTOR!

King and a woman who had been dropped and broken but had been put back together by the Master Himself. I went from a crawl to a stand, to a step, to a walk. Then, I began to soar! I stepped into my purpose and destiny by owning my truth, unlocking my voice, and becoming all that God created me to be. And. So. Can. You. "The champion within you will emerge victoriously."

BIO

Paulette Harper is an eleven-time best-selling, two-time award-winning author, speaker, certified empowerment coach, and expert story coach. She has been featured in CBS, ABC, The Sacramento Observer, CBN, and NBC.

Paulette uses her gifts to equip ambitious Christian women speakers & entrepreneurs to write, publish books, and be the catalyst for transformation in their spheres of influence. She is committed to empowering women and equipping them with tools to unapologetically share their voices and stories, as well as helping them push past barriers and discover their purpose so that they may become the best version of themselves.

As a minister of the Gospel, she has devoted her life to sharing the message of hope on as many platforms as possible. Paulette preaches, "Live with purpose. Don't limit God. Stay focused and allow God to take you places you have only imagined."

Visit Paulette at http://www.pauletteharper.com

RASHEDA HATCHETT, MN, RN

THRIVING THROUGH GRIEF: HOW I TURNED GRIEF INTO PURPOSE
BY RASHEDA S. HATCHETT, MN, RN

I was 13, and I remember it like it was yesterday. It was the day that changed my life forever. I came home from school, and my mom just wasn't herself; she was quiet, withdrawn, and stoic. I had never seen her like this before. She always greeted me with a smile when I came home from school. As my brother and I started our chores and talked about our day cracking jokes and laughing, she still didn't perk up, and it seemed that nothing we did made a difference, and she was completely detached from our presence. It was like she was purposefully staying away from us, and neither of us could figure out what was going on.

Later in the evening, it was time for her to go to work, and on these nights, she would leave us instructions for taking care of our baby sister, and she'd make dinner early so we wouldn't have to use the stove. But this day was different, there were no instructions, and the conversation was very different. Instead of the laundry list of do's and don'ts, chores that still needed to be finished, and reminders not to eat all the dinner and to save some for her, her instructions were about not answering the phone. My mom sat us down at the dining table, our normal family place of gathering and daily conversation, but not usually before she went to work. Normally she just hollered out her directions, asked if we had any questions, and reminded us to lock and put the stick in the door.

This time, as we sat at the table fearing we were in trouble for something because, as far as we knew, we hadn't done anything, but she was so distant that we were sure we had to be in trouble. As we looked at each other, waiting to find out what we had done and what the punishment was going to be, my mom said, "Don't answer the phone for anyone, I don't care who it is, do not answer the phone." We looked at each other in complete confusion and disbelief. "Why can't we answer the phone," I thought. I'm sure she could tell by the look on our faces that we were utterly confused. She left and just as she instructed, we didn't answer the phone. When she got back home, she called us back to the dining table. We sat down, and for what seemed like 30 minutes, we sat in silence.

Neither my brother nor I wanted to say anything because we didn't want to incriminate ourselves for whatever this punishment was, so we sat in silence. Finally, my mom said, "I have something I need to tell you. it's about your dad." I knew my father had been sick. That was no secret, I had gone to visit him the previous October, and at that time, he had full-blown lung cancer; he was really skinny and very weak.

However, he did everything he could to assure me that he was still the strong strapping superhero I remembered. My dad was an avid smoker; it wasn't uncommon for him to smoke a pack of Marlboro cigarettes every day. As a young girl, I found his smoking intriguing. He seemed so sure of himself and important with his work uniform, snapback hat, and a cigarette hanging from his lips. Once I got a little older, I tried to get him to quit smoking, and I would tell him how bad it was for him and how much God didn't like it that he smoked. He never got mad, he never yelled, he would always say, "Daddy's gonna quit soon." I believed him. On that visit, I can recall figuring out just how sick he was because all he wanted to eat was ice cream. He said it made the pain in his chest feel better. I didn't know a lot, but I did know that the pain must have been excruciating to eat ice cream all day and night.

I AM A VICTOR!

What I didn't know was that my superhero was slipping away right before my little 13-year-old eyes. After silence that felt like forever, she said, "Your dad died today." I honestly don't remember anything else after that. I didn't hear anything. I couldn't feel anything. I was numb. I remember crying and feeling crushed. I knew our late-night talks and his confiding in me about his troubles was over. I had lost my superhero. The gravity of my father's passing would manifest itself in ways that I couldn't ever have anticipated. I would see girls with their fathers and just breakdown. Every milestone he missed tore my heart out. As I grew older, that pain was exacerbated with every man that broke my heart, and I became harder to love because I closed myself off each time that pain reared its ugly head. I was the bitter young lady with more pain than I could deal with, but a heart of pure gold if I let you in to experience it. I began to turn on myself, and I hated what I saw in the mirror. I no longer felt worthy of even my own love. It would take years for me to regain a healthy relationship with myself and learn to love myself purely and genuinely.

Sometimes we reduce ourselves to our circumstances and position ourselves to receive far less than what God intended for us. That was me; after I lost the love of my life, my real live superman, I spent years looking for love in all the wrong places and finding myself tolerating abuse and self-sabotage. I spent so much time focused, obsessed even, with what I lacked and the things I thought I needed to be worthy of love and happiness. That's the thing about grief. It's not always about being sad or crying; much of grief is about how the pain of loss shows up in your life and changes how you see the world and yourself. Being consumed with stinking thinking robbed me of confidence, self-esteem, and my dreams. I was on the brink of giving up on living a happy and fulfilling life. I was tired, burnt out, frustrated, and simply surviving. It was time for a change. I needed life to be different, to feel different, and I realized one day that I was ready to be my own hero and walk in victory instead of wallowing in defeat.

I remember the day that I chose to pick myself up and live my life. I had just finished my master's degree and was so empty. I tried to fill my emptiness with accomplishments and accolades, and still, I felt completely alone, and the void I was trying to fill was now a chasm. Each day that I ignored the longing in my soul, it seemed to get bigger and more undeniable. It was time to show up for me and to finally allow myself to show up for me guilt-free. I began taking personal development classes, hired a business coach, took trips to sit at the feet of elders I desired to learn from, and permitted myself to be enough just as I am for those I am supposed to serve. The freedom that I created when I decided to put myself first opened my own mind to the possibilities that lay ahead; it illuminated what life could be like for those closest to me.

I began to share my journey, and people began to see the changes in me and wanted to learn how I changed my own life. This was when the world opened up for me. I had the unique opportunity to help other women bounce back from the brink of burnout and overwhelm, recover from the damage of grief, and position themselves as worthy and powerful. My work took shape, and my love for guiding inspirational visionaries to expand made all the pain of my past and all the lessons worth every second. I often tell people if you have the "Audacity to T.H.R.I.V.E. TM (Transform and Heal Resilient Inspirational Visionaries to Expand), the world will open up for you, and your purpose will flow from you like water, and you'll never be able to shrink again. My story isn't unique; tales of grief and pain are all too common. What makes me different is my desire to use my pain to help myself and others become the best versions of themselves possible and create lives that excite and fulfill them. My work with female leaders brings me the greatest joy, and I know my father looks down and is proud of how I used what he taught me about being present for others to help women transform and heal. I am a victor because I T.H.R.I.V.E.!

I AM A VICTOR!

BIO

Author | Speaker | Resilience Strategist | Resilience Based Leadership Coach | Entrepreneur

Rasheda opened Panacea Nurse Delegation Services in 2017, where she provides education, delegation, and consultation services to adult family homes in the greater Puget sound area. Rasheda Hatchett Media, LLC, is a coaching and consulting firm steeped in her passion for women's leadership and wellness.

Rasheda is an 3x author, dynamic speaker and resilience strategist and coach. Through her coaching and consulting firm, Rasheda is on a mission to coach female leaders from burnout and overwhelm to T.H.R.I.V.E. and confidently own their power. She is the creator of the "Audacity to T.H.R.I.V.E. ™" coaching program designed for powerful visionaries desiring to beat burnout and expand.

Rasheda is the mother of one son, two adult bonus daughters, and memaw to two beautiful grand-children.

Connect with Me:
Web: RashedaHatchettMedia.com
Email: Rasheda@RashedaHatchettMedia.com
IG: www.instagram.com/rashedahatchettmedia/
LinkedIn: https://www.linkedin.com/in/rasheda-hatchett-mn-rn-b50521196/

ANDREA HAYDEN

THE ME YOU DIDN'T SEE
BY ANDREA HAYDEN

THE STIGMA OF INVISIBLE ILLNESS...

Over 1 billion people worldwide live with some kind of disability, according to the World Health Organization. According to Forbes, over 42 million Americans have a severe disability, and 96% of them are unseen.

It's rare to see me without my statement jewelry and red lipstick. Yes, honey, if you encounter me in these streets, you would never imagine what challenges lurk behind my glam. For me, it represents protective armor from the people blinded by aesthetics.

THE BEGINNING...

In 1982, I graduated from a vocational high school in San Antonio, Texas, and earned my cosmetology certification. An eager 16 years old, I was ready to dominate as a professional hairstylist and future entrepreneur.

Just like a Sci-Fi movie, there was something awful lurking beneath the surface that would change the trajectory of my life. Two months into my budding career, my hands began to pain me so badly I could barely hold a comb, accompanied by unbearable ankle pain. Unbeknownst to neither my parents nor me, I had developed two invisible illnesses Lupus and Rheumatoid Arthritis overlap condition. With very little known about these conditions, I felt incredibly isolated, stuck at home in bed for days or weeks at a time. It was all starting to affect my physical and emotional health.

By my 18th birthday, I was encouraged to apply for permanent disability by my doctor. He said I would probably be wheelchair-bound by the time I was 30 years old. At times, what is meant for your harm, works for your good. I lost my mother at thirteen months old; born and partly raised in Brooklyn, NY, moving around living place to place gained me resilience, independence, and strength beyond my years. So, I quickly rejected the notion of disability and wheelchairs. I had my first apartment and was ready to live my best life! I pushed through the pain using my passion as the bulldozer. I learned quickly to focus on what you can do instead of what you can't and advocate for myself.

WHAT I STRUGGLE WITH MOST...

For years I stressed about debilitating fatigue affecting my work schedule. Every day I struggled, not knowing how I would feel. I dreaded having to call and reschedule clients. Because my illnesses are not obvious, some people did not believe, accept, or understand. As I reflect back on some of the most difficult health episodes over the years, I'm often disheartened to think about lying in ICU with life-threatening blood clots in my lungs or dealing with a three-month hospitalization due to a Brown Recluse Spider bite while worrying about my newly opened salon/spa with 12 employees. Sadly, upon my return, some of my clients never even asked how I was feeling... it was business as usual.

Living with an invisible illness is a double-edged sword. You are championed when you show up in service to others in your fullest capacity—but not extended that same grace when the complexity of living with an unpredictable multi-system disease inconveniently rears its ugly head. The comment of "you don't look sick" is not a compliment... it can be received as dismissive, disbelieved, and invalidating. Invisible does not mean imaginary; just because you cannot see it does not mean someone's not suffering. It will converge into every facet of your life, impacting your career, relationships, parenting, sleep, and social life.

I AM A VICTOR!

I am very aware that I don't look sick at times. But I work damn hard to achieve that momentary milestone of feeling strong enough to get up and get dressed. However, the emotional and psychological damage from societal and self-invalidation is severely impactful. The hardest part for me, hands down, has been the collateral damage of misjudgment by others. Being blamed, mistreated, and judged is demoralizing to people already suffering. It is not uncommon to feel threatened because "you don't look sick" to park in an accessible parking spot at the supermarket. Only to come out to find a handwritten note on my car that reads "Bitch, there's nothing wrong with you," or I arrived at the airport curbside for a wheelchair, only to be told, "You are too pretty to be in that wheelchair." At times, I want to scream... leave me alone; I'm battling my own body!

THE AWAKENING...

I am the person who goes the extra mile to personify excellence in all aspects of my life—at times feeling like I was losing my edge. This made me question my competency and capacity to continue operating at a high frequency. The decline in physical abilities was compounded by unpredictable changes to appearance caused by the disease itself. Medically induced skin issues, hair loss, joint damages, and particularly weight gain from steroids and other medications greatly damage one's self-esteem. I felt like my body's betrayal was slowly chipping away my confidence and self-worth. It may seem silly to some, but the day I realized I would never wear high heels again due to my ankle joint damaged... I cried like a baby.

Many conditions cannot be seen, including Fibromyalgia, IBS, Celiac disease, Chrohn's, and PTSD, to name a few. Over the 39 years since my first diagnosis, I have developed a total of (5) conditions... Lupus, Rheumatoid Arthritis, Graves, Antiphospholipid syndrome, and Raynaud's disease. The nature of these conditions are similar and unpredictable. The "flares" will come out of nowhere, with no rhyme, reason, or warning. Yet, on the surface, I look perfectly fine and therein lies the problem. Others will attempt to label you flaky and unreliable, so I have learned to set realistic expectations with business, friends, and family. These conditions can take a toll on relationships with customers, friends, and family. Many will write you off as unreliable or a hypochondriac, predominately due to an inability to participate fully in life.

LESSONS AND BLESSINGS...

I work, I play, and I live. All of which is done in relative normalcy and daily pain, depending on the day. I have the innate ability to push through enormous circumstances that would make some give up. God has yielded me the ability of high pain tolerance and a positive spirit to carry me through; many times, I have no earthly idea how I accomplish so much.

Despite 39 years of life's ebbs and flows, God has been so good to me. I have been a highly successful and recognized master hairstylist and hair loss expert. I've been a successful entrepreneur of multiple businesses for over 28 years. Now, I am honored to serve women like me who suffer from medically induced hair loss due to illnesses and medication.

MY DIVINE ASSIGNMENT...

Yes, I have internalized my emotions for many years. I wanted to be this super strong, super inspirational person. But I wasn't being transparent about my daily suffering; I learned to mask it well. With focused intention, I had to stop the negative self-talk and change the narrative for my life. I may pack a bag to visit but not stay...in that dark place of depression, anxiety, and fear.

Through all of the hardships and hurdles, I believe God tested me at every level to see if my spirit, determination, and focus were strong enough for my purposed divine assignment as the visual example positioned to help women radically redefine their lives. It would have made a tremendous positive impact early in my life if I had someone who could relate to my struggles without judgment. Positive energy

I AM A VICTOR!

and clarity are the main currency that runs my life now. Every day I keep my goals in mind and ration my energy protectively.

TODAY IS A GOOD DAY...

I consider this my second act, following an illustrious career. My legacy work has begun, advocating for self-acceptance, and unapologetically living the life I desire. The spirit of my work is influenced by my love of helping others, especially women beauty professionals and entrepreneurs. My focus is helping women amplify their voices and come off MUTE to advocate with urgency. They can redefine success by identifying their "NEXT" and utilizing skill sets and passions to discover untapped revenue streams while improving their quality of life.

I was once asked, "what do you want to be remembered for?" After much reflection, I pray my life represents "A story of one woman's 40-year battle with invisible illness; A story of resilience, strength, and determination, while using my voice to help others navigate through pain and perseverance, and ultimately invalidation to vindication.

WHAT I KNOW FOR SURE...

I can be brave and candid in opening up about my invisible illnesses. The conditions have taught me the importance of stillness. Because of them, God has gifted me with super-powers and a broader perspective. My illness might be invisible, but at five feet ten inches of fabulousness...I will never be! If you still have breath in your body, you too have the opportunity to radically change your life!

BIO

Andrea Hayden, founder of The Hair Management Group, has 39 years in the Cosmetology, Hair Restoration and Trichology industry. Essence magazine listed her as one of seven hair loss experts in the country. As the past Director for the International Association of Trichologists USA, she oversaw all operations to include establishing the U.S based World Trichology business conference.

Andrea is known as a change agent and master collaborator with an abundance mindset. She is the trusted resources for women beauty professionals and solopreneurs seeking to identify their "NEXT" while utilizing skill sets and passions to discover untapped revenue streams, while improving their quality of life.

Andrea was awarded The Marlene Hansen Award from the International Association of Trichologists and San Antonio Business Journal recipient of the Women's Leadership Award in the Inspirational Leadership category.

*Featured co- author (March 2021) Beyond 2020: Life and Business Lessons on Thriving Amidst a Pandemic

I AM A VICTOR!

REGINA KENAN-LADY LION'NESS

LADIES IT'S TIME TO SOUND THE ALARM
BY REGINA KENAN-LADY LION'NESS

"Some women get erased a little at a time, some all at once. Some reappear. Every woman who appears wrestles with the forces that would have her disappear. She struggles with the forces that would tell her story for her or write her out of the story, the genealogy, the rights of man, the rule of law. The ability to tell your own story, in words or images, is already a victory, already a revolt."
Rebecca Solnit

When life hit me, it hit me hard, like a ton of breaks, and I did not think that I was going to make it because I did not think that my voice mattered, nor was I strong enough, so I had to cry out to God and ask for his help and his guidance. See, I am a mother of three beautiful children, two boys and a girl, and the grandmother of three beautiful grandchildren, two boys and a girl. I lost both of my sons to the prison system two years apart, my oldest son was sentenced to life with no possibility of parole in 2008, and my baby boy was sentenced to 23 years in 2011. That alone is enough for any mother to lose her mind. I started having anxiety and panic attacks, and I did not know how to control them or what to do about them. I didn't think that anyone cared about what I had to say because of what was going on in my life with my sons. I was embarrassed and ashamed, and I blamed myself. I fell into a dark depression, but I realized that I had to pull it together because I had another child at home, and she needed me to be strong for her, so I had to lean on my heavenly father to get me through because I could not let my baby girl down.

While going through all those trials and tribulations, I knew that I had to seek God's face because there was no way I could make it without him. God sent my daughter and me a spiritual family, and with their support and love, we were able to get through it. I thank God for my church family because, yes, there were days that I wanted to give up because it was too much for one mother to deal with on her own while trying to raise a child alone. I had to put my emotions and feeling behind me because my daughter needed me there to help her get through school while dealing with losing both of her brothers to the system, the only male figures that she had to look up to was gone.

I felt like I had failed my children. I blamed myself for an exceptionally long time until one day; God had to sit me down and explain to me that it was not my fault what happened to my sons. I had done what I was supposed to do, and I did a great job raising my kids, and that is when I decided that it was okay to go on with my life and not feel guilty about it. See, when life's trials and tribulations hit you, you tend to throw in the towel and give up, and that is what I did. I did not allow myself to be free to live the life that God had in store for me.

Unfortunately, while going through all of that, I was vulnerable, and I allowed myself to get into another domestic violence relationship yet again. I had hit rock bottom yet again and allowed the devil to come in and send someone into my life to fill a lonely void, so I thought. In three months, he managed to convince me to move out of the home that I had just moved into, so me and my daughter ended up homeless for three months because he promised me a new and bigger house... Lies. That man stripped me of my happiness, voice, home, self-esteem, and dignity, and I almost lost my daughter.

Thank God my sister let her stay with her because I did not want her to see what was going on with her mother. I felt like I was not worthy of being loved or having happiness. I had settled, and that is not what God told me to do. I allowed this man to take me away from my family, church family, and my ministry. He took my credit cards, my

I AM A VICTOR!

cell phone, he shut me out from the outside world, and I had to sneak and purchase a prepaid cell phone so that I could call my godmother. She was the only one I knew I could talk to that wouldn't judge me or call me crazy, but I had to hide it when he was there. The freedom that I once knew was gone in three short months.

It was the worst three months of my life. I prayed and asked God to take my life because I did not want to live like that anymore. I felt like I was in a losing batter. Because he was a minister, I felt like no one would believe me, and he was an influencer, and I didn't believe that my voice meant anything to anybody because I didn't know very many people outside of my church. As women, especially women of God, we must be there for one another because we are a sisterhood. I am dedicated to bringing women together and building a community of women to empower one another to do more and be great at what we do.

I have had many obstacles to distract my life that could have stopped me from doing what I know God has called me to do, but I know my mission, and I know my why and because of that is why I do what I do. I must let my voice be heard by doing God's will and helping women because I had no help on my journey in life.

God has put me on this earth to minister to women worldwide and encourage, empower, and educate them about using their voices to build an empire for themselves and their families. The trials and tribulations that I had to endure was not for me. They were for the women that I will meet on my journey, and I am excited about this journey that God has me on, and I cannot wait to meet those phenomenal women. Ladies, it is time for us to stand up and take our crowns because it is time out for us being silent. We will no longer be silenced. We will sound the alarm and let our voices be heard in a powerful way while helping empower, educate, and encourage other women that we meet on this journey of success. I know my assignment is to work with these women, and I will help as many women as God sends my way. I must help them to build up their self-esteem, courage and let them know that you can be on assignment and multitask at the same time because I do it every day by taking care of my two grandchildren while my daughter works. I have multiple businesses that I manage, I am an author, speaker, fashion designer, publisher, and funeral planner, and I mentor and coach women daily while operating my personal businesses, all while homeschooling my 6-year-old grandson and taking care of my 1-year-old grandson so no excuses ladies you must fulfill your dreams and do what you have been called to do. We are standing up and taking our crowns this year and reaching out to women globally to help other women do the same thing. Ladies, you must know your self-worth and do not let anyone tell you that you are not beautiful, powerful, and intelligent because millions of women are out there just like us, and they need to be heard. I am on a mission to serve women all over the world to know their potential.

My vision is to help women and young girls become more comfortable speaking in front of groups and share their opinions, all while building up their self-esteem. I mentor and teach them how to create a vision for their families and their businesses and to help them to understand that they have the potential to achieve more than they believe they can.

BIO
Regina is the mother of three and the grandmother of three. Regina is a motivational speaker, author, entrepreneur, and Founder of Heart To Heart Connections Publishing Co., Kenan Funeral Planning Services Inc., and Lady Lion'ness Boutique. Regina is a domestic violence advocate, coach and mentor and the owner of Lion'ness Royale' Travels Travel Agency.

She has an AAS Degree in Fashion Design & Merchandising from Katherine Gibbs School. She's a co-author of "I Survived It," "From Employee To Entrepreneur", "When We Pray," "Courageous Enough To Launch", "Breaking The Code", "I Am A Victor and "A Mother's Love" Raising Kids in a Pandemic.

I AM A VICTOR!

She is the founding member of The League of Girlfriends Leadership Academy and the Captain of The League of Girlfriends of WNY & Tri-State Area Chapter.

Contact info: ladylionnessden@gmail.com
Social Media Handles:
Facebook: ReginaKenan-Ladylionness
Instagram: ReginaKenanLadyLionness
LinkedIn: Reginakenanladylionness
Twitter: ladylionness3
YouTube: Let's Sound The Alarm

INGRID LAMOUR-THOMAS

I AM A VICTOR OVER HYPERTHYROIDISM AND GRAVES' DISEASE!
BY INGRID LAMOUR-THOMAS

As for you, I will come with healing, curing the incurable, declares the Lord
Jeremiah 30:17 (MSG)

On March 12, 2020, I was sitting at the doctor's office waiting on my lab results. The doctor came in and said, "Ingrid, what happened to you? What happened to your blood tests this year? Your numbers are all over the place. I do not see you for a year, and you come back with such drastic lab results. What is going on? What has been happening?" Indeed, I was experiencing some stress in my life, my finances were not in order, and I was in the middle of taking a new direction with my life. She proceeded to explain how my TSH levels were high, way above the normal range, and that it might be hyperthyroidism/Graves' disease. She had me schedule another appointment to get blood drawn in two weeks for a full thyroid panel to get further results and better evaluate my thyroid gland function.

Next appointment, I came back to obtain my results, and she said, yes, it is confirmed. It is Graves' disease. I said I do not receive that word (I will live and not die). She laughed. No, you are not going to die. Graves' disease is named after the Irish physician who described this form of hyperthyroidism, she said. She explained that some of the symptoms were heart palpitation, weight loss, hair loss, among others. I told her no wonder I was experiencing heart palpitation for the past couple of months. I even saw a cardiologist who cleared me of any heart disease or ailments after a full cardiac workup. I told you there was nothing wrong with your heart, he said, your heart is perfect.

I was left with no clear reason why I had heart palpitation of over 100 times per minute. All-day long, I could hear the whooshing of my heart beating in my ears, WHOOSH, WHOOSH, WHOOSH. And when I lay my head on my pillow at night, I could hear more clearly the rapid beating of my heart on the pillow, BOO-BOOM, BOO-BOOM, BOO-BOOM. All. Night. Long. BOO-BOOM, BOO-BOOM, BOO-BOOM. To the point where I would want to put my hands over my ears and yell, "leave me alone!." See, I barely had a good night's sleep in over a month at that point.

My doctor assured me that it could be treated with either surgery, medication, or both. Anyway, I will give you a referral to see an endocrinologist who specializes in treating the thyroid gland, she said. The first time I saw the endocrinologist, she was very worried about how my thyroid felt while consulting me. I will never forget the worried look on her face. She had me complete a few tests to rule out throat cancer and surgery. The first round of tests was inconclusive. She was not too satisfied and therefore was not able to draw a conclusion. I proceeded to have a biopsy, which is done by inserting five needles in my throat. I was scheduled to come back in a month after all the tests.

Within that month, my appearance was already changing. I lost weight, at least 10 pounds, and my eyes started to cave in. I looked sick. I knew I had to take action and find natural treatments to tackle this diagnosis. Right away, I started asking questions to know what kind of "monster" I was dealing with. My doctor assured me that this is something that can be treated with medication. I was not satisfied with being able to treat it with medication. I wanted to know if I could treat it naturally. Therefore, I started to research what hyperthyroidism and Graves' disease were and what lifestyle you must live to experience your breakthrough and healing. I started taking vitamins &

supplements such as Selenium, Ashwagandha, Zinc, Vitamin D, etc. After one month, I started feeling better. I went back to see the endocrinologist, and she no longer had a worried look on her face. She said I looked better and wanted to know what I've been doing differently. I told her I started taking vitamins and supplements. She said, continue doing what you're doing. It's working for you. That was my first win.

Hyperthyroidism is an autoimmune disease. Autoimmune means your immune system is attacking itself. Your immune system is attacking your healthy cells by mistake. In the case of Hyperthyroidism/Graves' disease, your thyroid is attacking itself. There are multiple types of autoimmune diseases: Lupus, Celiac disease, Crohn's disease, and others. It is important to point out that although each autoimmune disease is different, they are mostly triggered by stress, some stressful events, such as pregnancy, death, separation, divorce, etc....

There are two autoimmune diseases related to the thyroid: Hyperthyroidism/Graves' disease or overactive thyroid and Hypothyroidism/Hashimoto or underactive thyroid. It is said that hyperthyroidism is much harder to treat than hypothyroidism. Medication is often necessary to control hyperthyroidism, but certain foods, vitamins, and nutrients also help return your thyroid function to normal. Hyperthyroidism has multiple symptoms: heart palpitation, unintentional weight loss, hair loss, muscle weakness, excessive or frequent bowel movements, bulging eyes, goiter, or swelling of the thyroid gland. I started to display all these symptoms except goiter.

To maintain a healthy thyroid, first and foremost, you must eliminate stress and its triggers; change your diet (plant-based worked for me); exercise (low cardio); lift weights to keep muscles strong and remain positive. If it is not treated effectively, it can lead to nutrient deficiency in the long term. It is important to maintain your thyroid healthy; therefore, you must support your body with the nutrients overactive thyroid depletes.

In September 2020, I completed my six months follow up and a new round of labs. My doctor said to me, Ingrid, I commend you. You did it all by yourself. You did it without my help. You did it without medication. You did it through your own research. Your thyroid is perfect. Your numbers are back to normal. Now I know I did it with God's help, not just my own research. I thank God for his faithfulness, his grace, his blessings, and his love. I thank God for giving me the wisdom to research this diagnosis and how to treat it naturally, for giving me the fortitude to implement everything that I learned and for giving me the strength to remain consistent every day, and finally, for giving me a chance to see my life changed for the better and witness health rise in my body. It's a kiss from God.

In conclusion, I want to share how I overcame hyperthyroidism/Graves' disease and experienced my breakthrough to total health and wellness. Here are ten decisions I took and implemented to treat my thyroid and nurse it back to its normal function.

1. Ask questions!
Your doctor is there to help you understand your diagnosis, your treatment plan, your lab results, your next steps, etc... Come to your appointments ready to ask questions and acquire knowledge and clarity regarding your diagnosis and action steps.

2. Research. Educate yourself!
Read articles. Read books on autoimmune diseases. Research online.

3. Become your best health advocate!
Learn how to read your lab results by asking your doctor to give you a better understanding - Always request a copy of your medical records - Seek a second opinion when necessary – Ask questions – Do not allow to be rushed through your appointments.

4. Exercise!
Low cardio exercise routine and weights to keep your muscles strong.

I AM A VICTOR!

5. Change your diet!
Ex: Plant-based – Gluten-free – Paleo etc.… Find the diet that works for you (plant-based worked for me) - Reduce iodine in your diet – Vitamins – Supplements

6. Drink plenty of water!
Always hydrate.

7. Choose an Anti-inflammatory diet!
No sugar – No processed foods – No caffeine – No soda – No chocolate – No fried foods (get an air fryer) – No alcohol.

8. Manage the underlying causes!
Stress – Trauma – Hormones shift – Separation – Divorce etc...

9. Reframe your mindset and your words!
Words kill, words give life; they are either poison or fruit – you choose. (Proverbs 18:21 MSG).

Do not claim the disease. Do not say you have hyperthyroidism. I never did. For example, the doctor said…, the doctor sees… or I am dealing with hyperthyroidism.

10. Remain positive!
Do not give in to the disease. Remain strong. Push yourself even when some days you do not feel like doing any activities, do it anyway. You can do it. Like me, you can turn your thyroid function around to normal.

Disclaimer: I am not a doctor. I cannot diagnose, cure, or treat anything. This is only for educational purposes. I am merely sharing a regimen that worked for me.

Nothing that is mentioned in this chapter is intended to replace your doctor's consult and medical advice.

BIO

Ingrid Lamour-Thomas is an international motivational speaker, 4x Amazon best-selling author and the founder of The Green Light Movement, LLC. which empowers successful, professional career women approaching or over 40 who feel stuck, behind, and are wondering about their purpose, that it's not too late to boldly chase their dreams without hesitation.

As a Confidence Strategist and Image Consultant, she helps women become more confident by looking great on the outside while feeling great on the inside so they can show up bolder, put their best foot forward and go after what they want while looking chic!

Ingrid is also the founder and CEO of Beloved Children and Family Services Foundation, Inc., 501(c)(3) nonprofit organization serving both her homeland, Haiti, and her community in Orlando, Florida. Its mission is to provide services, education, nutrition, and basic life necessities to children from low socioeconomic communities.

IG, FB & Clubhouse: @IngridMotivates
https://linktr.ee/thegreenlightmovement

I AM A VICTOR!

VALERIE K. LEWIS

A SMILE THAT COULD KILL
BY VALERIE K. LEWIS

I remember the day my aunt and I decided to take my seven-year-old daughter to the park. We had recently moved to Texas. I was hurt, broken, and reeling from a recent break-up. Sitting quietly with my aunt, watching my daughter happily play was the peace I needed. Our solitude and focus was soon interrupted by the presence of a charming and friendly gentleman.

He had a beautiful smile, and just to let you know, I am a sucker for pretty teeth. We talked and talked – about what, I don't' remember, but it was uplifting enough to stop me from thinking about my ex during the conversation. Needless to say, I had a great time talking, listening, and laughing with him. After a while, we decided to leave, and as we said our goodbyes, he ran over and said, "I enjoyed myself. Can we exchange numbers and continue the conversation?" I said "yes," and we did. He didn't let it end, though, with the phone exchange and surprised us by saying, "I live right down the street, I cooked, come to my apartment and eat." My aunt and I looked at each other strangely and indicated that it was not a good idea. He said, "I am not going to hurt you, come on we will have a good time." My aunt whispered to me that she had her gun in her purse, so we went with a little hesitation.

We danced, ate, yakked, relaxed, and had a good time. The clock ticked, and before we knew it, 11:00 p.m. had arrived. It was late, time to leave and get my daughter home. Little did I know that my life would soon change.

We talked every day after that initial encounter. He wanted me to come over, but I did not want to go over there alone, so I told him, "not right now. Let us still work on getting to know each other." I was still hurting from my past relationship, yet I was starting to be attracted to him. He showed so much interest in me; I was liking and needing that attention. I was in a vulnerable state, and I also had low self-esteem. No one could have guessed my inner state of being, but I knew. We continued our daily phone conversations, and he eventually asked me on a date. I was fine with that because we would be in a public place and not at his home. I do not remember the restaurant, but we had a great time. When you first meet someone, you always show the best of you.

The relationship progressed. I finally went to his place. Everything was still going well. I left that night, giving him my first kiss. From that night on, he started to show his true self to me in subtle ways. After our date, he started calling me more. When I did not answer, he would say, "when I call you, you are supposed to answer," and he would jokingly laugh. Sign number one; I did not catch it. I told him, "I was busy," and he said, "I missed you. I really wanted to hear your voice." Sign number two; I did not catch that sign either.

Looking back, I realize that all he wanted to know was if I was home and not out with someone else. Fast forward, we got married. The time came for him to openly show who he was: abusive - verbally, mentally, financially, physically, and sexually. During the time of abuse, I was pregnant; I always tried to keep him calm because I did not want to jeopardize my pregnancy, but that did not matter. I remember one time when I was pregnant; he hit me in the head and started yelling at me about what I was cooking, and I became scared, frustrated, and angry. I threw a knife, and it just missed his eye, literally. In the midst of our toxicity, I thank God I still delivered a healthy baby girl. Life continued.

I AM A VICTOR!

He would take me to work and pick me up. He made sure to get there early enough to see who I walked with, exiting the building. He would call me on my breaks and make sure I was on the phone with him the whole time. He controlled the finances, taking my check. I know you are asking, "Why did I stay?"

I was raised in a two-parent household. I wanted both my daughters to experience the same upbringing. I also felt that I needed a man to validate me, even if it meant accepting the violence. My low self-esteem coupled with needing validation from a man and co-dependence had me settling for any man. My thought was it is better to have a piece of a man than no man at all. But one day, I decided differently.

I decided to leave. The deciding factor -- he tried to kill me. One evening we were coming from a party, and I fell asleep. He had pulled over on a bridge where there were no lights nearby, and he slapped me in the face. This shocked me awake as he pulled me out of the car, cursing, saying I was going to die that night. I surreally saw the reflection of the moon on the water as he was attempting to throw me off the bridge. I fought with all my might. Everything was happening so fast. I was hanging from the bridge, pleading, and begging God, "please, God, do not let me die."

Suddenly a police car pulled up, and my husband ran. He got arrested on some other charges and served time. I never pressed my own charges. God saved me; that is where I pressed into my life. I knew I needed to get my life together for myself and my children.

You see, I had to work on my inner self and my mindset. I had to learn how I should feel about myself, so I would not repeat the same cycle. I was raised in the church, so I knew to call on God during my domestic violence and to follow his spirit. The words of the prophet Jeremiah 29:11 comforted me, telling me that God had plans to comfort and profit, not harm me. I had a future. At that time, I didn't know why that scripture was in my spirit so deeply, but now I know. I know now that God can use me to help other women because of what I went through.

I no longer need validation from a man; that part of me is over. I do not have to show all my goods to get attention from men. God is my validation. I do not need a man to be happy. I am beautiful, intelligent, bold, royalty, a queen, powerful, and an overcomer. So are YOU! Never let anyone validate who you are. Know who you are, walk with your head high and stroll into your purpose.

Let me share what I did to start my life over because I had to deprogram myself. I moved in with my sister-in-law for a little bit. I went back to church to get God's Word on the inside of me. I learned what God had to say about me. I prayed daily and volunteered at the church. I went to a support group; that really helps. I started being around positive women and connected with women who were entrepreneurs. I stayed in the company of powerful women who, in turn, empowered me.

I eventually moved to the other side of town physically, mentally, emotionally, and spiritually! I spent more time with my children, putting them first. I got a better paying job, and I started my own business. I spoke positive affirmations to myself. I forgave myself. You have to forgive yourself. It is not your fault that someone else cannot manage their own behavior and demons. I love baths, and I would take a bath every night, relax and smile because I finally learned to dwell in peace.

I did not smile much during that period of domestic violence. Now I appreciate the importance and value of a smile. Jeremiah's promise is for you too. You can have peace, joy, happiness, confidence, and all that life has to offer. Remember, love does not hurt, and it is never too late to be what you might have been. It is your time to be free; so, smile, friend, your future is bright!

I AM A VICTOR!

BIO

I am a wife, mother, grandmother, entrepreneur, podcaster, film writer and co-author. I am the founder of a Non-Profit Organization called 'You Don't Have To Cry Alone In Silence. We help Domestic Violence victims and survivors with their necessities transitioning from the shelter to their new residence. We empower provide support and inspire them to live their life to the fullest after domestic violence. I know from experience that you can heal, have peace, confidence, and love who you are again. You can become the strong women that you were born to be. I knew from my High School years that my purpose in life was great. My mission is to bring awareness about Domestic Violence and help those who are hurting and suffering in silence. Love does not hurt.

Website: http://www.youdonthavetocryaloneinsilence.org
Facebook: facebook.com/ydhtcais
National Coalition Against Domestic Violence: www.ncadv.org

LAURA LOUIS

COUCH TO PODIUM: BECOMING A PAID SPEAKER
BY LAURA LOUIS, CEO OF COUCH TO PODIUM

As a man thinketh in his heart, so is he (or she)

As I was sitting in a business workshop at my church, Word of Faith, I saw Dr. Alduan Tartt, a psychologist. I was so nervous about approaching him. In my mind, I thought to myself, "His platform is huge" I recognized him from television and radio as well. Have you ever felt nervous about approaching someone because you felt their platform was so much larger than you could ever imagine for your own? At the time, I was fresh out of graduate school and trying to find my way.

I told myself, "Laura, you only need 60 seconds of confidence". I walked up to him, and I said, "I admire your work, and I would love to collaborate with you." To my total surprise, he was open to it. He called me the next week. He allowed me to join him in speaking at the National Sales Networker Conference (NSN). They wanted a male and female team, so I said, "Yes." I knew that there are times you just need to take a leap of faith, and God will take care of the rest. I knew I had a gift, and despite my nervousness, I wanted to be compensated for sharing my knowledge with others. When speaking to the VP of the association, I asked to be paid for a recording of my speech and my travel expenses.

Sidebar, always negotiate. After all, what do you have to lose? At least, shoot your shot. Understand, you will not always get 100 percent of what you ask for as a speaker, but one thing is for sure, as my grandmother would say, "a close mouth doesn't get fed." Meaning you never know what is available until you ask. Negotiate a win-win. Over the years, I have learned you must give yourself permission to be the CEO of your life, and this starts with coming up with a clear, detailed strategy to achieve your goals.

Now, fast forward to the day before my corporate keynote talk.

I am at the venue, getting ready for my soundcheck; while going through my presentation, I look behind me, and there is Brian McKnight. He was also doing his sound check for the next day at the very NSN conference that I am preparing for. I literally wanted to pinch myself. It was at that moment that I realized my gifts were making room for me all along. I want you to know that when you step out on faith, God will open a door for you to enter that money can't buy. Take the step, and God will do the rest.

It was August 7, 2014. I was headed in to speak on one of the largest stages I had ever spoken on.

I thought to myself...

I am on stage with well renowned Dr. Tartt, world-known artist Brian McKnight and life-changing, motivational speaker Les Brown, "How did I get here? Do I have what it takes?"

My anxiety was through the roof. It was time for me to walk on stage, and I was reminded that Les Brown would be the next speaker. The pressure was on; my throat started to close up, and then came the bubble guts.

Have you ever had a moment when questioned if you were built for this?

I AM A VICTOR!

I reminded myself of the years of preparation for this moment. The years earning my Bachelor's Degree, completing my Master's Program, and the nights I stayed up writing my dissertation for my Ph.D.

At that moment, I knew I had to build up the courage to stand and deliver at the National Sales Network Conference because they were writing me a check. I said a quick prayer as I always do before speaking. At that moment, a speaker was born. All of my nervousness went away.

The only thought that crossed my mind was that I may be the only couples' therapist some of these salesmen ever see. The divorce rate is high, and I am responsible for giving couples hope that their marriages can be transformed. Each one of us has a purpose. Always remember, YOU are someone's answered prayer.

I have done over 1,000 speaking engagements and traveled to over 20 countries, including Paris, Greece, London, Brazil, Spain, Dubai, West Africa, Morocco, Vietnam, and my favorite, South Africa. My work has been featured in NBC, PBS, Reader's Digest, and The Wall Street Journal. As much as I love counseling couples, I realize speaking allows me to transform marriages worldwide.

Now, I have the opportunity to help other business owners share their stories. It excites me when I get messages from my clients telling me about the conferences they have produced and the money they have made as a result of working with me. Speaking has gained my clients more exposure and credibility in their business. They now know the steps to craft a great pitch. I teach them how to stand out by giving them the hidden secrets on how to position their message in crowded marketplaces. You have to know how to market your story as a speaker. My 15 plus years as a speaker has taught me how to market any business.

It is my desire to not only share my story, but I also want you to walk away from reading this with some key nuggets on how you can book speaking engagements. If you follow these key steps, you will be well on your way to building a solid speaking business.

If you would like to book paid speaking engagements, consider these five steps to get started speaking:

Be clear regarding your signature story and your brand: Great speakers have a great signature story that aligns with their overall brand and business. This alignment is crucial because it allows you to earn money based on your personal journey.

Identify your market and develop your pitch: Determine who needs your services and what makes your business useful to the market. It is important to know why your service is necessary. What expertise do you bring that is more valuable than the next person? Paid speakers pitch an offer. Sell your story. Do this over and over again. Flood your target market. Your market may be corporations, conferences, colleges, or churches, whoever can benefit most from your story. It is also important to follow up after you reach out. I recommend following up at least 7x. This can include phone, email, and I even have social media strategies for engagement. If you need support with creating an irresistible pitch, check out my Couch to Podium Academy at www.CouchToPodium.com, where I walk you through step by step how to create your pitch and how to follow up.

Start developing brand assets: To be taken seriously as a speaker, you need a video reel with testimonials. Do a brand photoshoot (whenever you are asked to speak, people want photos to create flyers to promote you). A great look goes a long way.

Share a picture of you speaking on stage with a call to action for people to hire you. Once you have booked a gig, hire a photographer and videographer to cover your major speaking engagements. You can start small but make sure it is professionally done. This will help build social proof when you share about places that you have spoken.

HARO - Join Help a Reporter Out. If you want to gain more media exposure, use this tool. Journalists use this daily to seek resources for story segments, and when you subscribe to you will receive emails from reporters looking for experts. Sending messages that answer their question exactly is one of the keys to getting your media idea picked up by the journalist. You must get to the point quickly in your response.

You have the power to change lives as a speaker, but you will have to own your voice and recognize the gifts you have inside you. If you're able to connect with your audience, bring your story to life and touch them in that place that makes them move, it will be the key to someone's breakthrough. You were meant to shine. There is a purpose in your testimony. Don't sit on your gifts; you do not have time. Your time is now. Stop waiting to be chosen.

How I help speakers share their story

If you want to be a member of an AMAZING community of speakers and business owners and receive exclusive access to someone who has spoken all around the world, join the couch to podium academy at www.couchtopodium.com. I am here to support you. We are winners. I teach speakers how to unapologetically share their stories with the world. Let's take the victory lap together.

BIO

Being a professional speaker is beyond what is just presented on the stage. Consequently, many speakers struggle with monetizing their message during these current changing times. Understanding how to market is the key to booking speaking engagements. Dr. Laura Louis teaches you the behind the scenes blueprint on how to book paid speaking engagements. She has conducted over 1,000 speaking engagements nationally and internationally. Dr. Louis has been featured on NBC, Wall Street Journal, PBS, Readers Digest, Cosmopolitan Magazine, and The National Sales Conference. Dr. Louis is the founder of the Couch to Podium academy which consists of Courses, Retreats, Seminars, and a Mastermind. If you are purpose-driven entrepreneur with a desire to discover the business side of speaking visit www.couchtopodium.com

I AM A VICTOR!

NICOLE S. MASON

INFIDELITY DID NOT WIN, LOVE DID!
BY NICOLE S. MASON

From the outside looking in, one might get the impression that my husband and I have always been as happy as we are today. But, if the person with that thought were honest, they would have to admit that all relationships have their ups and downs, ins and outs. However, I am here to tell you that infidelity almost wiped this relationship out! Before I go any further, it is important for you to know a little bit about how it all started.

You see, I met my husband the very first month I stepped onto the Howard University campus. What attracted me to him, from the onset, was his beautiful 1000-watt smile. And, of course, he had plenty of game. Lord knows, don't tell him I finally admitted that his "rap" game was tight. LOL, He tells the story to our sons about how his words had me falling all over him, but the reality for him, it was love at first sight.

I'm writing this story, so I get to tell my version of it. LOL In any event, I will admit that there was instant chemistry between the two of us. He was unlike any other man I had ever dated. He was going somewhere, and he was pursuing his education in college and not on the streets. Whew, Chile, that is another topic for another book. But, in any event, there we were, I was 17 years old, and he was 18. Young, hopeful for the future, full of vigor, experienced, or so we thought, and love gripped our hearts. Oh, and did I forget to mention, we were arrogant, selfish, and we both wanted to "have our cake and eat it too?!" So, you won't get the wrong idea here, we all have the good and bad, the yin and yang, the positive and negative in all relationships. You get the picture.

Love can be tricky, with lots of twists and turns. It can have you so high in the sky one day and try to pick yourself up from the lowest pit the next. But again, this is the reality of life. The dichotomies of life can wear you down if you spend an inordinate amount of time trying to keep your life on one side versus allowing the balance of it all to show you what you are really made of and to learn the lessons and appropriately apply them to your life. Well, my newfound love and I were getting ready to experience this roller coaster ride that we know as life, love, victory, defeat, I'm out of here, I can't live without you, I'm over this and you, I forgive you and let's keep working on it… It makes my neck hurt now thinking about how much we have gone back and forth, but this back and forth is par for the course to get to a place of what I will call confident, can't nobody come between this, try to infiltrate if you want to kind of love!

We had our first son when we were 19 and 20. Much too young to start a family because there was still so much to learn about life, one another, and how we would make a living to take care of ourselves. Thank God for our families. It is safe to say that most girls mature much faster than boys. Of course, this is not an absolute. But, for my relationship with my then-boyfriend, it was indeed the case. Becoming a parent early either makes you grow up, or it causes you to dig your heels into your young life and act a plum fool, as the elders would say in my community. Immaturity certainly doesn't help the matter. I was moving forward in my college matriculation, and he was playing basketball and sleeping with every girl, seemingly on and off-campus.

Now, before you go judging me on why I didn't leave him, let me tell you. I left him and did my share of cheating, but that didn't help the situation at all. Although we were hell-bent on "getting each other back," our love for each other was much too strong to keep us apart. We also had people in our lives coaching us and mentoring us through the rough times we experienced. Let me stop right here to tell you about one of our cheerleaders: my dearly beloved grandmother. When I tell you that she gave every young man I introduced to her the absolute blues! LOL, She would look them up and down and give them a once over and look me dead in the eye and say, "Oh no." Sometimes, it would be right in front of them. She did not have any "cut cards" about how she felt about people, situations, and matters. Edna Mae Maynard was a shrewd businesswoman who had migrated to Washington, DC, from South Carolina with my grandfather in the 1940s. They opened a dry cleaner, and my grandmother was in business for more than 50 years before her retirement. She knew people. She had keen discernment, and she just was not shy about sharing her revelations.

When I introduced her to my now-husband, she gave him a look over and immediately said, "I like him. He is perfect for you." Chile, when I tell you, I almost passed out. I couldn't believe what I was hearing. This was a critical moment for me and what would soon turn into a major turning point in my life – work to overcome the hurt and pain of the infidelity in the relationship looming large or fight for the love we felt and what the unknown future held for us. Based on the words of a woman I knew loved me and had my very best interest at heart, I chose to give the relationship everything I had and trust the process that love never fails! Not only was my grandmother right; she lived to see us grow together and blossom into a loving couple, taking on the world, TOGETHER!

The other people who were very instrumental in helping me to navigate the twists and turns in my relationship were my parents. Although they were divorced, they both loved me, and they really liked Sean. My father approved of him when he met him, too, just like my grandmother. It took my mom some time to really warm up to him. She was fiercely protective of me. When it was all over, said, and done before my mom passed away, my husband and my mom were extremely close. I share this to offer to you that you need people in your life to help you navigate the tough spots in your relationship. You need people who can see the good in both people and not just the parts they want to see. You need people who will tell you the truth about your bad decisions and wrong choices. Trust me, the people in my life did not sugarcoat matters, and they were not in the business of mincing words or holding back the truth.

I can tell you that it still took us some time to get on one accord with our lives. My then-boyfriend turned husband had two children before we were married. A guy I was cheating with was shot and killed in my car. Time and space doesn't allow me to unpack all of that, but the message that I want you to breathe in deeply is this - a relationship can survive infidelity if the two people want to make it work, agree to work together to make it work and then does just that – work at it.

My husband and I have worked diligently on our relationship. We got married when I was 27, and he was 28. The two people must also continue to work on themselves individually. This is why people should not enter into marriage haphazardly. It can be rough terrain and a smooth road, all at the same time. You must be intentional about commitment, dedication, discipline, communication, vulnerability, respect, honor, and, more importantly, love. I am reminded of Proverbs 10:12, "Hatred keeps old quarrels alive, but love draws a veil over every insult and finds a way to make sin disappear." (The Passion Translation)

We have been together for 34 years now. We've been married for the past 24 years. We have three sons and two daughters. We have one Sugarbaby (my name for my grandchildren) and one Sugarbaby on the way. The good has far outweighed the bad. "Love is large and incredibly patient." (1 Corinthians 13:4 TPT) I AM A VICTOR! YOU CAN BE A VICTOR TOO! Infidelity Did Not Win, LOVE DID!

I AM A VICTOR!

BIO

Nicole S. Mason is an international speaker, executive leadership coach, attorney, and best-selling author. She is dedicated to helping high achieving women reach their next level in life by creating the success they really want, so they realize their greatness personally, professionally, spiritually, and financially!

Nicole is a trailblazing senior leader for a Federal Government Agency, serving as the first African American woman in her position. With a very bold and confident spirit, Nicole is intentional about pushing and provoking women to Show Up Great, Speak Up with Confidence and Stand Out with Courage.

Follow Nicole on all social media platforms @nicolesmasonesq. You may also visit her website at www.nicolesmason.com. To join her mailing list, text SHOWUPGREAT to 22828. If you would like to reach her via email, you may send an email to nicolesherronmason@gmail.com. Please put I AM A Victor in the subject line.

LAKISHA MCGANEY-OSEI

LIVE. MOVE. OVERCOME. COME GET SOME.
BY LAKISHA MCGANEY-OSEI

Are you ready to Live? Are... you... ready... to Live! One more time for the people in the back, so busy doing, that they don't have time being.

I have three questions for you as we journey together across these next few pages. It may seem obvious at first, "why of course I want to live," I mean, who does not want to be out here living their best life, right? But are you really living your BEST life? Are you living out your dreams, your passions, your destinies? Or are you overwhelmed with the facade that you have grown to masquerade in? Surely there must be room for us to LIVE! There must be room for me to L.I.V.E.

"I'm staring at it. Enough of putting my hands on it, but no heart in it. Enough of wasting time and talents. Evicting everything that is not productive in my life... My wheat(talent) will outgrow, outlive, outdo my tare. My brokenness is my blessing. It's transition time, unapologetically."

This was a summary of my Facebook status on January 7, 2018. Have you ever asked yourself, how did I end up here? A few weeks ago, my mother was telling my son, "I didn't have much trouble out of your momma; she was always about getting her books." Now why, one may ask, would that make me tense up slightly? In those words were the reminders of me as a young girl that I needed to do the right thing, I needed to be good, I needed to be the one who graduated from high school and be the first in my family to go to college. Don't get me wrong; I understand there is nothing wrong about wanting the best for your children; however, that meant me being determined to figure it out on my own, neither of my parents had the privilege to experience college life. And I did not want to disappoint them or me by not being able to accomplish this feat.

You see, I realized a few years ago that I spent most of my young adult life trying to make sure that I was doing the right thing to keep peace and keep face. This translated to my personal relationships as well. Even when I knew early on that marriage was not going to make things better, it appeared to be the right thing to do, right? I mean, I had just celebrated graduating from college with my second degree. At the time, my advisor asked me why I was not applying for PT (Physical Therapy) school. I remember the next words so clearly, "what are you going to do instead, get married and start a family?" Initially, I was like the gall of him. No! I said boldly and confidently (with no clue I was already with child). Not even a month later, it was confirmed, I found myself pregnant with my first child and married by that fall. I didn't know everything would change so quickly, but I knew one thing this baby was going to live, and I would bring forth life. Are you ready to L.I.V.E.?

"Your time is limited, so don't waste it living someone else's life. Don't be trapped by dogma – which is living with the results of other people's thinking."
Steve Jobs

L.
Love yourself unconditionally.
There is nothing that I am more grateful for than the birth of my three children. Let's make that emphatically clear—each one born 3 to 4 years apart during some trying times. I remember people would say, wow, you spaced them out good as if it were planned, not knowing there was one who didn't make it for each that did. I have only said that out loud to one other person in my almost 48 years. There was shame in what I had done; I mean, how could I? You feel alone and

lonely, whether it is a joint decision or not. There are decisions that we make throughout life that haunt us and those that heal us. Either way, you have to L.I.V.E. with the consequences of those decisions. You have to Love yourself unconditionally through it and grant yourself the self-compassion that you grant others. I am not here to justify or testify. I am here to amplify the one who is beating themselves up right now literally and figuratively, because of a decision they made or did not make. To the one who has stopped living, because you are questioning how somebody can love me after this or that. It is you that I come for. The heartbroken, the trampled upon, the fallen, who forgot to Love yourself unconditionally. The judgment that is cast upon us is not for us to consume. Get up, let's go. You can't bring forth life if you refuse to live. It's time to Move. Are you ready to M.O.V.E.?

"You have to learn to get up from the table when love is no longer served."
Nina Simone

M.
Make your mark.
It is interesting how our perception of ourselves can limit our production. Previously I mentioned how our decisions can haunt or heal us. They can also halt or catapult us into our next. Nothing happens without making a M.O.V.E. first. As an athlete (I don't believe you ever eliminate that out of your blood, so I won't say former), I played many sports growing up, but hands down, basketball was my first love. I even had the opportunity to play a couple of years in college. As a power forward most of my career, I learned very early that unless I made a move, nothing was going to happen. You literally got yelled at for sitting in the paint. You had to decide to cut across the middle, drive to the hole, or at least pivot hard. Pause right there. Did somebody say pivot? The year 2020 had people thinking that pivot was a new word, a new concept. What I have learned over this life is that if you are going to make a mark, you are going to have to make a move. The ball of opportunity is being passed around, and there is always

someone waiting to pick your pocket. But know this, it only takes a quick second to make the move that will change your life forever. I stayed in the paint for over a decade and was literally holding myself hostage and did not even know it. So, 2020 saw me finalizing a divorce decree that had been hanging over my head. Release yourself to pivot and take your best shot. Are you ready to Overcome?

"Three things in life - your health, your mission, and the people you love. That's it."
Naval Ravikant

O.
Operate from the Overflow.
When I came across this quote, I had to familiarize myself with who made such a poignant statement since I could not recall ever hearing this individual's name prior. Well, Naval Ravikant is an Indian-American entrepreneur and investor known for the AngelList and investing early in prime stocks such as Twitter, Wish.com, Poshmark, Postmates, Thumbtack... well, you get my point. So, in other words, he is a man of great monetary wealth.

Why is this of importance, you ask? Because even at the end of the day, it doesn't matter how much WEALTH you have or don't have, HEALTH is what sustains you no matter how large your bank account. In essence, live life full out and make your mark. Health and wellness is a passion of mine. Not only is it a passion, but I also believe that it is the mission I was created for. How we manifest our mission is unique to us. My ability to draw in the right people at the right time and collaborate for the greater good is why I founded the Wrapped in Wellness retreat. The very theme for this year, Meet us at the Well, alludes to the overflow that is to exude from honoring our health, mission, and the people we love. After you make your move, to make your mark, you have to remember why and how you came to operate in the overflow. You were an overcomer, plain and simple. I am an overcomer. My decision to live, move and overcome is not just a cute

I AM A VICTOR!

play on my initials (you caught that right?); it is how I permitted myself to be the best version of myself. I am not defined by the children that I did not bear, nor the marriage that ran its course, or the monetary stature I have yet to reach (and I mean yet). What ultimately defines me is the love, impact, and overflow from which I operate. Today I encourage you to live your best life. Live. Move. Overcome.

BIO

Lakisha McGaney-Osei is a Holistic Health and Wellness Coach, and Founder of Joy is Just Over Yonder, LLC, providing health and wellness experiences through her signature events Wrapped in Wellness and Journey2Amazing with Coach Lakisha. In 2019 she began her health and wellness show Let's WRAP About it Wednesdays, to interview upcoming and seasoned coaches and wellness professionals across the country. She has a passion for helping women over 40 embrace self-care, self-love, and self-compassion through their journey2amazing by walking it out herself. She holds certifications in Reflexology, Level I Reiki. I Touch Soles introduces reflexology to those who look like her. A two-time author already, she is looking forward to the release of 4 book projects just in the first half of the year including two of her own.

Contact Coach Lakisha at http://www.joyisjustoveryonder.com/ or hello@joyisjustoveryonder.com
Follow us on insta/twitter @iamlmosei
Follow us on FB @journey2amazing @joyisjustoveryonder @itouchsoles

STEPHANIE L. MCKENNY

IT HAPPENED SO FAST
BY STEPHANIE L. MCKENNY

It happened so fast. She received her diagnosis, went through surgery, radiation and then rang the bell. We were so excited about her finally ringing the bell in July 2018. Before we had time to really celebrate, the cancer moved to another area in her body. This time it was in her lungs.

I will never forget the look on the doctor's face when he told us the cancer had spread to her lungs. My daughter cried and left the office, but I remained questioning him about what we could do next. He suggested we go to Charleston to MUSC, but his look told it all. The only thing is, at the time, I didn't quite understand it. I was hoping for the best, but his look told me he already knew the outcome.

At the time of my daughter's initial diagnosis, our relationship was not at its best. Our relationship became estranged shortly after my second marriage. I can remember driving back from a doctor's appointment for my dad when my daughter called me. She was crying hysterically, and I heard her say, "They said I have cancer." I said, "Okay… well, cancer doesn't mean death." I was trying to reassure her that it didn't mean that she had to die. I believed that when I said it, but there obviously was another plan. I'm not blaming God for my daughter's death. Today, I'm thankful that she surrendered her life to God, and she made it to Heaven. That is my consolation through this entire process.

My daughter, Crystal, went through a ten-hour surgery inside her mouth, and part of her skin on her thigh was placed on her arm and in her mouth. The surgery went well. She was resilient, strong, and full of life. She was determined to fight this cancer and win. She constantly confessed, "I'm already healed." Her faith was not always strong throughout her life, but she managed to come back to God after her diagnosis.

In September 2018, she began chemotherapy for the cancer that was found in her lungs. I can remember so vividly the day we went to MUSC to begin the process. It was September 6, 2018, and we were in the treatment room, and we talked and laughed like old times. We even thought about a product that we could create for women that day. We laughed about it, but we considered pursuing it (who knows, I may still do it).

I'd heard that chemo was difficult for some people. I know it attacks your immune system, and it wears on the body. Well, that's exactly what happened to my daughter. She got one good dosage, and her body reacted in so many negative ways that she was really only able to get one more and one other treatment of immunotherapy. She was in and out of the hospital from September to December 2018. I know this may sound strange, but we had good hospital visits together. We talked, laughed, and reminisced about things. Often, the nurses would come in and check in on us to see what was going on. See, no matter what happened in our past, we loved each other.

I want to share a few things in this chapter to help you on your journey towards being a victor. Listen, amid all the chaos that may occur in your life, you can come through with the victory. I preached a message last year entitled, "Your setback is your comeback." God will use the very thing that set you back as a springboard that will lead you to your comeback.

I AM A VICTOR!

First, I want to share about my estranged relationship with my daughter to help those experiencing issues with relationships with their children and/or parents. I had my daughter when I was a teenager. I was actually 15 years old. I was a freshman in high school. I didn't know anything about sex, protection, or love. I was truly sheltered by my parents and naïve to boys, but somehow I fell for the words of her father. When I got pregnant, I didn't tell my parents initially because I was planning to abort her. However, I couldn't find the money, and it became too late. I remember the day when I was lying in my parents' bed, talking to my mother, and she noticed that my stomach was big. She scheduled a doctor's appointment and found out I was five months pregnant, which was too late to terminate the pregnancy. My father was upset, and I felt like I let my parents down.

This is where the feelings of shame were planted in my heart. Let me tell you; shame will stick its head up and show up in various ways in your life if you've experienced it and don't confront it. Previously, our family discussed adoption, but I couldn't do it. When I saw Crystal, I remember crying and telling my parents I could not put her up for adoption. My father immediately said, "We will do what we have to do to raise her. I won't separate a mother's love for her child." So, we all brought Crystal home from the hospital. She was biologically my daughter, but my parents loved her so much that she and I were like sisters in their eyes. I had some amazing parents, and they loved my daughter like their own. Crystal and I were close, almost inseparable. When you saw me, you saw her. I loved her, and I still do.

As I mentioned before, our relationship became estranged after my second marriage. I will not go into detail about all that took place, but I will say that it is so important not to allow unforgiveness to remain in your heart. Not letting go of the past mistakes in relationships will hinder the future of it. My daughter found it difficult to forgive me. I found it difficult to forgive myself for some choices I made. The forgiving and not forgiving cycle ran its course until the day she told me she had cancer. I actually thought she hated me, and I kept allowing it to eat at me. I had to finally forgive her and forgive myself. Later, I found out that she really loved me and just wanted her mother… period. After her death, all I kept saying was we missed so much time dwelling on the past that we couldn't properly create new memories. I want to encourage mothers and daughters… forgive and love. Love and forgive. You need each other. Let go of the past mistakes, pain, and the things that have been done or said to love each other. If either of you leave this earth, you will wish that you had, and time cannot be turned back. Resolve it today.

No one wants to bury their children. It is the most difficult thing to do. I used to hear about people losing their children, but I never thought it would be my experience. I felt alone, and I felt as though no one understood my pain. It's a different pain from losing an aunt/uncle or even a parent. Losing what you gave birth to is hard to adjust to. Wow, as I write that, it resonates something in my spirit. Sometimes what you have birthed (not necessarily your child) doesn't quite work out. Sometimes you lose it, sometimes it fails, but don't give up. You have so much more to birth. You are a victor by nature, and you must press forward as I must.

In the midst of it all, I'm learning so much. Death will teach you about life. If I had a choice, I wouldn't have wanted to learn some things this way, but I am learning. This is what I want to share with you as well, learn something through the process of reaching victory. The process will teach you some things about yourself and about what's in you.

The last thing I want to share is that your experiences will turn purposeful. There is a reason for everything, and there is a purpose for it. As a result of losing my daughter, I am working on turning this experience into something purposeful. My daughter went through so much with dealing with her battle of cancer that I saw that some serious needs went unfulfilled because of her sickness. She couldn't provide for herself or her four children because of it. Because of what I saw, I have recently started a non-profit in her honor to help those who are dealing with cancer and domestic violence. The name of the non-profit organization is, Connections Impacted by Grace CDC. Your experience will be purposeful. Use what you have gone through to impact lives positively.

BIO

Stephanie L. McKenny is a native of Montclair, New Jersey. She received her license to preach in August 1993. She moved to South Carolina where she works with her husband in ministry. She has three children and four grandchildren.

She conducts an annual women's conference (Pearl Sistahs Conference), facilitates workshops/conferences for women and teen girls. She has recently established her first non-profit organization, Connections Impacted by Grace Community Development Corp (CIGCDC).

She graduated from Columbia College in Columbia, SC and has completed her graduate studies with a Masters in Counseling at Webster University.

She is an author of over ten books and the owner of J & J Publishing Company and Creative Vision Productions, LLC a self-publishing company aimed at assisting authors with publications, play productions and product creation. You can contact her for speaking engagements by emailing her at: slmckenny@gmail.com. She can also be found on Social Media (Facebook/Instagram and Twitter)

CAROL T. MULETA

I'M FIRE-PROOF
BY CAROL T. MULETA

"There's too much smoke!" Those four words jolted me upright from a deep sleep. I jumped out of bed and lunged across my studio apartment and jerked the door open. The voices in the hall had spoken the truth – smoke was billowing down the hallway, insistently pressing the walls in search of a breach. I could taste it. I could hear the faint buzzing sound of an alarm. Our building clearly was on fire. Running on adrenaline by now, I slipped on some shoes and grabbed something to cover my pajamas and dashed out to the hallway. Where were the men attached to those voices I heard earlier?? I was on my own. I raced down the seemingly endless hallway upright but quickly realized I should be crawling and ducked below the haze. In decades past, our 4-story building had been a hotel with an antique elevator (definitely, a no-go now) and, thankfully, a wide elegant staircase leading to the front lobby. As I sprinted down two landings, I suddenly sensed things were getting hotter where I was headed. I stopped. I looked to the large windows on the stairwell. I peered out and saw a narrow space between the building and an ornate iron fence. I couldn't see a way to easily clear that fence without seriously injuring myself. I also feared getting stuck between a burning building and a fence designed precisely so you couldn't climb it.

I just started crying. I screamed, "Jesus, help me!" I was out of options. Suddenly, a man's voice told me to come upstairs. Upstairs. In a burning building. Are you kidding me? He started pleading with me. Reluctantly, I came upstairs, and he led me to the fire exit I had unknowingly run right past and led me down the dark stairs and out to safety. Once outside, I would learn that this man had already led his family safely out of the fire and had come back inside. I never found out why he returned, but I'm sure thankful he did.

After the fire was extinguished, we were surprisingly allowed to go back into the building. The lobby stairs that had originally figured into my plan of escape would soon become a crime scene. A bitter ex-boyfriend had set a fire at the door of his beloved's apartment AND at the bottom of those stairs to ensure that she couldn't escape. But she did. Thankfully, he, too, was unaware of the emergency exit. I made my way back to my apartment, and the very first thing I laid eyes on was my Bible. I felt convicted because I had fallen off in my study and communion with God. As I reflected on the previous few months, I could see I had clearly lost my compass.

The journey leading up to this harrowing night began with a move to a new city a year and a half before. I'd been captivated by the prospect of a flourishing romance and a promising career in fashion merchandising. I had a brand-new car and was living on my own for the very first time. It all started so well, but by year's end, I had neither of the things that attracted me to this town. My relationship failed, with no small amount of drama, including betrayal along with emotional and physical pain. My dream job turned out to be pretty dreary after all. When the year-long training program came to an end, I knew I needed to find a new place to work. Now, I stood in front of the mirror; my face layered in soot streaked with tears. My prized white trench coat was now a smoky gray. It was tempting to think God had surely turned his back on me. BUT alas, he *had* brought me out of that fire. And, though I couldn't fully appreciate it then, He'd already rescued me from a future that promised heartache and disappointment, personally and professionally. He'd also shielded me from injury when my car skidded and crashed on a rainy expressway as I drove to work, narrowly missing entanglement in a tragic pileup right ahead of me. God had been VERY good, and most importantly, He had never left me. I, on the other hand, was a pretty fickle companion to Him at the moment.

I AM A VICTOR!

Thankfully, I had seen the handwriting on the wall at my job and had already landed a new government position by the time my manager and I sat down to talk about my future at the company. I walked out of that meeting, departing on my terms. My start date for the new job was about 30 days out, so I cooled my heels doing some temp work, so I could still eat. God was with me.

> *"Consider the ravens: they neither sow nor reap, they have neither*
> *storehouse nor barn, and yet God feeds them. Of how much more value*
> *are you than the birds!"*
> Luke 12:24

The new job gave me a place to land while I figured things out professionally. The fire shed light on other changes I needed to make. Like, why was I still living in a place where the rude and reclusive property manager ignored my calls for maintenance AND neglected to tell me about the emergency exit?? The next day I headed down the street to check out a newly renovated apartment I had noticed earlier that week. I interviewed with the owner and signed on the dotted line. Next, I marched into my property manager's office and announced that not only was I breaking my lease and leaving ASAP, but I was taking my deposit with me. In the next breath, I cited my litany of grievances with him and the property owners. And just like that, we had a meeting of the minds, and I left just like I said I would. God was with me.

I only moved down the street, but it felt like a world away. As soon as I got there, I finally followed through on my plan to pursue a graduate degree. I discovered I needed two prerequisites for most of the M.B.A programs I was considering, so I immediately enrolled at a local college. By then, I'd hit my stride with my new job – I was managing a $17 million inventory program, supplying naval air facilities around the world, and earning accolades and bonuses for my performance. Finally, I took on a part-time job for extra money to eliminate all of my debts. I gained admission to some of the leading business schools in the country. You know I picked the best. And God went with me.

210

Since those early days, I have continued to walk through situations that are too hot to handle, intact. Here's what I learned along the way:

Make time for God. Your faith and His wisdom will come through for you EVERY time. He knows what came before and what you will face ahead. If you pay attention, you'll see He's leaving clues all the time. He will make provisions for you. In the face of insurmountable obstacles, He's inclined others' hearts to show me favor that they nor I expected. And He will do it for you if you invest in a relationship with Him.

Follow your dreams. It is good to connect with people and take in new experiences, but don't get sidetracked. Stay focused on your vision. You better believe those around you are focused on theirs. Diligently gather the tools and skills you need to bring your vision to fruition.

Don't get too comfortable. Even when you think you've made it, stay vigilant. Your circumstances can change in an instant, and you've got to be ready to move, or to escape, if you need to.

Know your options. Options equal opportunities. Sometimes, there's more than one way to get where you want to go, but purpose will lead you to the right option. ALWAYS operate in purpose.

Don't get stuck. Life happens, and it's not always pretty. Don't wallow in WOE is me. Get ready to walk in WOW, it's me!

As I conclude this chapter, we are wrapping up 2020, a year we will never forget. There was fear, uncertainty, and unspeakable suffering as we faced down the formidable foes of the coronavirus, racial tensions, and economic despair. In moments like these, I have been forced to become rational, resourceful, and resolute and to put on a coat of courage to walk through the fire and get to the other side. God is with me... I'm fire-proof.

I AM A VICTOR!

"See, I have refined you, though not as silver; I have tested you in the furnace of affliction."
Isaiah 48:10

BIO

Carol Muleta is a Parenting Strategist and Consultant, and creator of The Parenting 411, a portal where she engages parents through webinars, private consultations, and the Parenting 411 radio show. When frustrated and discouraged parents work with Carol, they get their JOY back. Together, they create a parenting philosophy that complements the personality of each child and restores order in the home, so Moms and Dads can BREATHE, and each child can reach their full potential. She was named 2019 DC Mother of the Year® by American Mothers, Inc. Carol received the Radio Personality of the Year Award at SpeakerCon 2019. She is a contributing author of the riveting anthology, <u>Courageous Enough To Launch</u>. Carol is also the author of an upcoming book, <u>Mother's Work: Pearls of Wisdom & Gems from My Journey</u>. Carol and her husband are proud parents of two young adult sons. Connect with Carol at www.carolmuleta.com.

EMMA NORFLEET-HALEY, PSYD., LCSW, LICSW, LCSW-C, CAMS I

TRIUMPH OVER TRAUMA
BY EMMA NORFLEET-HALEY, PsyD., LCSW, LICSW, LCSW-C, CAMS I

Join me if you will on a personal journey. A journey that entails a brief but thorough overview about the need to remove your mask where "Trauma" is concerned. I will tell my story using Who, What, When, Where, and Why my trauma occurred. Trauma will be defined to ensure your understanding of this term. Trauma research entails physical manifestations, but emotional trauma (in my view) can be equally paralyzing. Masked trauma unresolved will manifest in ways that will prevent living your best life. As I share the Who, What, When, Where, and Why about my trauma, you will not believe the transformation before you to date. In other words, I do not look like my story. As such, I intend to inspire, promote, and encourage others to work through unresolved trauma.

It is important to share statistically how not alone I was regarding coping with trauma. For example, the number one cause of death from ages (1 – 46) is "trauma" (Data retrieved from NCIPC, 2015B)? Another alarming fact is the annual cost of trauma ($671 billion) in health care and lost productivity" (WISQRS, CDC, NIH, MEDICAL NEWS TODAY 9/21/15). Now, not only are these statistics alarming, but they drive my mission to help other victims with unresolved trauma.

The (WHO) in this story includes my deceased father, mother, baby sister, and brother, as well as my living three older brothers and four older sisters. My late father (WHO & WHAT) was a functional alcoholic, and we called him "Dr. Jekyll and Mr. Hyde." During the week (Monday through Friday until 5 pm), my father could be described as a quiet man (Dr. Jekyll). However, if drunk by the time he arrived home Friday nights, the emergence of Mr. Hyde shortly followed. We all knew the imminent risk was upon us as my drunken father would unleash holy terror to all in his crossing over the next two days. Just imagine dealing with such terror during your vulnerable and formative years (ages 1 through 8).

The next "WHO," my late mother, bore the brunt of my father's weekend drunken rages until it turned toward my older siblings. Witnessing verbal and physical altercations between one's parents is very unsettling and confusing at any time, but especially during formative years. Entering school and hearing other kids talk about their fun weekends with their fathers added to my confusion. And in hindsight, that early peer exchange marked the evolution of me masking trauma when interacting with peers.

Unfortunately, and unbeknownst to me at that time, my mask would change over the years. As I matured, I noticed the change in my mother and oldest brothers' mindset. They had grown weary of our father's (Dr. Jekyll and Mr. Hyde) weekends filled with a reign of terror. My teenage brothers maturing verbally and physically, as can be expected, began to challenge the harshness of the alcoholic. The oldest brother's fierceness can be likened to becoming laser-focused on protecting his mother and siblings from that alcoholic. An ongoing prayer for me at that time was for this alcoholic not to come home Friday nights.

As years passed, my father's drinking increased and offered no relief of fear for me on weekends. And just as you were becoming desensitized to the relentless physical trauma, the emotional trauma of witnessing such was taken to another level. Again, the brunt of his physical abuse was toward my mother and older siblings. However, in addition to physical and emotional abuse, another form of abuse just as heinous was on the horizon.

One late night when my mother was working at her second job, my drunken father attempted the most unthinkable and despicable act against one of my older sisters. He reached an all-time low in his alcohol addiction, and this was more than my courageous, fierce, and protective oldest brother could bear. Said brother foiled the father's attempt to sexually abuse our older sister by bursting in the room and confronting my drunken father. Although this was a needed interruption on my sister's behalf as my father pinned her down, none of us were prepared for what came next.

The interruption sent my father into a rage no one was familiar with. The rage was significantly worse than his previous rages. My father yelled and hurled verbal threats toward my brother, but there was no backing down in my brother that night. The father was met with stone defiance and resolve by my brother to save our sister from being sexually abused. My brother's undeniable confrontation and relentless resolve to stop this unconscionable sexual attack against our sister enraged my drunken father all the more.

In response, the father yelled and screamed alarming verbal threats. Haunting words invaded and intruded my thoughts for years after this incident. I will never forget hearing and watching my drunken father yell and stumble in haste toward the closet where he kept his gun. "I will kill you, keep standing there, you Son of a B-t-h, let me get to my gun." And my father's diverted attention from my sister gave her just enough time to free herself and run.

My fierce brother had saved my older sister but was now faced with saving the rest of us because in all the chaos, yelling, and confusion, my out of body experience was over, and I desperately needed to be rescued from it all. My father's drunkenness at that time was both a curse and a blessing. The curse entailed an attempted sexual assault, the threat to kill my brother, and shooting at us. The blessing in my father's addiction that dreaded night was that the alcohol-impaired his equilibrium and allowed my brother time to hurry us across the street into the woods, and no one was shot that night.

However, entering the woods for safety was short-lived. I recall vividly the sound of bullets whisking past our heads; as the fierce brother momentarily kneeled down amidst the danger, I heard the most comforting words "I got you, baby girl, it's gonna be okay." I then felt the firm clasp of my brother's hand squeezing mine and pulling me to safety. I remember the twigs/branches sliding on/about my face, chest, and legs in the woods. Given that there was no time to put shoes on, the ground stubbles and brows poked tiny holes in the bottom of my feet as my brother dragged me 2 ½ miles to the safety of my late maternal aunt's home. This most horrific and scariest time in my life took place "WHEN" I was five- or six-years-old living in "WHERE" Sharp Point, North Carolina.

The "WHY" as it pertains to trauma. Trauma is defined medically as bodily injury, wound or shock: The psychiatric definition is a painful emotional experience, or shock, often producing a lasting psychic effect and, sometimes, a neurosis." (Webster Dictionary, 1986). Several reasons explain my trauma; however, my father's addiction (if I had to name one) explains the "WHY" best. Alcoholism is a disease that does not discriminate and contributes to many sleepless nights during the first 13 years of my life.

Resiliency in a child is amazing, and I can personally attest to such. Equally important to my resiliency during the childhood trauma was the support of my family. I also had community support that included select teachers, guidance counselors, and close family friends. However, what happens if you do not have a primary or secondary support system?

I AM A VICTOR!

The above question will forever drive and fuel my mission to help powerful women cope with unresolved trauma to live their best. You can start by removing the mask of repression, denial, sadness, nightmares, and flashbacks, all of which could lead to serious mental health disorders (Posttraumatic Stress, Generalized Anxiety, & Major Depressive Disorders), to name a few. In closing, Trauma-Focused Cognitive Behavioral Therapy will provide a safe therapeutic haven for you to "REFLECT, REJECT AND RESET" your mind. Haley's Mind of Care Services, LLC offers quality mental health services to include seasoned clinicians' above evidence-based practice. Contact HMOCS, LLC via www.hmocs.org Office#: (240) 429-5390: Cell (240) 423-4109 if you are ready to "TRIUMPH OVER TRAUMA."

BIO
Emma Norfleet-Haley, PsyD., LCSW, LICSW, LCSW-C, CAMS I is the President/CEO of Haley's Mind of Services, LLC (an outpatient mental health agency). She is a trained mental health expert and Co-author in Dr. Cheryl Wood's upcoming "I Am A Victor" book to be released on April 13, 2021. Emma Norfleet-Haley and her other clinical staff provide a therapeutic environment that encourages, inspire, empower, and share ways to "TRIUMPH OVER TRAUMA," using evidenced based practices to include Aaron Becks (Cognitive Behavioral Therapy) J. Cohen, E. Deblinger and A. Mannarino's (Trauma Focused: Cognitive Behavioral Therapy) & S. Minuchin (Structural Family Therapy). She also facilitates professional trainings/workshops for mental health clinicians needing Continuing Education Units (CEUs) for licensure renewal. You can reach Emma Norfleet-Haley at her agency website www.hmocs.org; work#:(240)429-5390 and email: info@hmocs.org.

Social Media: @HaleyMindReset or norhaley1 (Instagram)
facebook.com/emma.norfleethaley

TANYA Y. PRITCHETT

EMOTIONAL NOURISHMENT
BY TANYA Y. PRITCHETT

Tears are streaming down my cheeks as I take a sip from the glass of red wine I'm holding. Suddenly, the water starts flowing faster, and my silent cries grow louder and louder until I'm screaming at the top of my lungs! No words, just screams. I look at the glass and want to throw it against the wall. I take a breath, then say to myself, "Tanya, who is going to clean up that mess? You're the only one here." My husband and I just separated; I could no longer deny my feelings.

"Show no emotion, feel no pain." I'm not sure who said it, but that has been my philosophy for most of my life. The only problem is, I do feel pain. I feel disappointed. I feel angry. I feel sad. Too many feelings and emotions are unraveling. Here I am, left alone with my feelings, and all I can do is scream and cry. It's what happens after spending a lifetime denying my own feelings and not expressing my emotions.

Reserved is what my teacher called it. In junior high school, I struggled to write an English paper about a personal characteristic- being shy. It had been several weeks, so I decided to talk to my teacher about it; otherwise, I would have no paper and fail my class. "I'm struggling to write about being shy.," I said. She replies, "You're struggling because you're not shy. You're reserved." That took me aback. There's a distinction between shy and reserved? I always just thought of myself as being shy.

Looking up the definitions, I found:

- Shy - easily frightened away, timid

- Reserved - slow to reveal feelings, thoughts, or emotions

It is true; I am slow to reveal my feelings, my emotions, and the thoughts connected to them. Reserved. I have a new personality.

Identifying a new personality reminds me of one of my favorite movies… Sybil. Sybil is a story about a young woman who had Dissociative Identity Disorder (DID) and 16 personalities. I connect to her because I have different personalities in different situations. I'm outgoing as a cheerleader; I'm nerdy when tutoring other students, and I'm reserved when needed and don't share my feelings or emotions.

As with many people diagnosed with DID, Sybil disconnected from herself and connected to each personality as a unique individual due to the traumas she experienced. Although not as severe, many people find themselves disconnecting from their feelings and emotions when experiencing traumas, and I am one of them. One of the traumas I experienced as an infant contributes to my being reserved.

My mom was very sick after I was born. My grandmother was there caring for me when my aunt called and said my uncle had been called off to the Vietnam War and she needed help with her two kids. A few days later, my grandmother arrived at my aunt's house. When my aunt got home from work, she heard what sounded like a baby crying and asked, "What's that noise?"

"I brought Tanya with me. Brenda's sick and recovering, and Jerome has to work. They didn't have a babysitter or anybody to watch her." My parents didn't come to get me until two years later; why, I don't know. By then, I had come to know grandma as, well, grandma, my aunt as mom, my cousins as my brothers, and my uncle, who was back from Vietnam, as dad.

I AM A VICTOR!

As an infant, I experienced the trauma of being disconnected first from my birth parents and then from those I had been programmed to know as my parents and family. That first night at home with my biological parents, my mom told me, I stood at the door crying, crying, crying because I didn't know where I was and didn't know who she and my father were. She said she tried holding me, but my father said, "No, it's good for her to cry it out." That was my first trauma, where I learned that my cries go unheard when I express my emotions.

You may not think that is traumatic. However, studies have shown that the first seven years of a child's life are the most important for their learning and personality development. Our brains are our central processing units (CPUs). Like a computer's CPU, our brains need to be programmed; this happens in our early childhood years. We learn by observing the people and situations around us. By two years old, my CPU had been programmed to disconnect from those I love and suppress my emotions when my cries go unheard. "Show no emotion, feel no pain."

Denying my feelings worked pretty well for me through elementary, middle, and high school, college, and even into my young adult life. Other traumas came, and with them, I recalled my early programming and suppressed my feelings. My uncle said to me one time, "You are just so nonchalant about everything," and I took pride in that; that I didn't cry in front of people; that I didn't share my emotions. At the same time, part of me always felt like something was missing because I didn't have deep, personal relationships and connections that so many people around me were having.

I thought I had found that missing piece when I started dating my husband. He wouldn't settle for "I'm fine" when asking how I'm doing. He'd ask more questions such as, "What are you thinking or feeling and why?" in his attempt to connect to me more deeply. Slowly, I started opening up and expressing myself to connect to him. However, after we married, we started having some marital problems.

Our discussions and arguments got so heated at times that I felt like my feelings and cries weren't being heard. I retracted to my old programming and didn't express my emotions so I wouldn't feel that pain.

But, like Sigmund Freud says, "Unexpressed emotions will never die. They are buried and will come forth later in uglier ways." My uglier ways came forth with food and alcohol. I became an emotional eater, which led to me being 40 pounds overweight and huffing and puffing when doing simple tasks like walking down the stairs. Although I learned how to nourish my body through diet and exercise to lose excess weight and improve my health, I still couldn't nourish myself by expressing my emotions.

I thought I was fine… until… that day when…
…he left.

Tears are flowing faster, and my silent cries that, for so long, went unheard are getting louder and louder. I have all these buried, unexpressed emotions inside and don't know what to do with them. I am alone with my feelings, and now my cries really are unheard. I didn't want to fall back into the habit of eating and drinking the feelings away. I was in a car accident soon before he left, so that I couldn't exercise and dance the feelings away. I did the only thing I could.

I SCREAMED, I CRIED, and I PRAYED!

"God has not given us the spirit of fear." I didn't have to fear my feelings. I showed my emotions. I felt the pain, and I'm a VICTOR because of it. The missing piece wasn't connecting to my husband; it was emotionally nourishing and connecting to myself.

*****

I AM A VICTOR!

Separation from your family, spouse, or job, a car accident, a death, or a worldwide pandemic; whatever the trauma, it could lead to feeling disconnected from others and yourself and cause you to bury your emotions with TV binging, overworking, or emotional eating. As with weight loss, there's no cookie-cutter solution. Here are three things I did that may help you get the proper emotional nourishment you need:

1.   **Give yourself permission to feel.** I admit there are times when I still struggle with putting emotions and feelings into words, but now, I'm more AWARE of them. Rather than being in denial, I acknowledge them.

2.   **Seek support.** Therapy helps me name and own my feelings and identify triggers when I start denying and suppressing them. Therapy provides guidance, support, and a safe space to let the tears flow.

3.   **Keep a gratitude journal.** I found victory in connecting with my feelings and nourishing my emotions, not with food but with gratitude. Write at least three things you are grateful for each day, including your feelings.

Keeping a food and emotions journal along with support from a health coach, like myself, may also help you be a VICTOR over emotional eating if you struggle in that area. I can provide guidance and support you through your weight management journey to improving your health. Go to the link in my bio to schedule a complimentary "Emotional Nourishment Call."

Remember, it's important to express your emotions not only to connect to others but, most importantly, to stay connected in a loving and nourishing way to the most important person in your life- YOU!

BIO

A multi-talented woman who has conquered her own weight challenges, Tanya formed TYPs4Life, LLC. to coach busy professionals to do the same. Using empathetic listening, attention to detail, her knowledge and experiences, Tanya CREATES convenient plans that allow them to RELEASE unwanted weight, INCREASE productivity, GAIN the vitality and confidence to do what they TRULY love without spending hours in the gym or kitchen!

As an Independent Affiliate, Tanya markets natural products and integrates those into her consulting based on the client's needs.

Tanya is Certified by American Fitness Professionals & Associates as a Nutrition and Wellness Consultant, Holistic Nutritionist, Weight Management Specialist and Sports Nutritionist. She is a Project Management Professional and has Bachelor's and Master's degrees in engineering and telecommunications.

Tanya is in Toastmasters, enjoys dance, photography, travel, and spending time with friends and family.

Go to https://linktr.ee/typs4life to visit her website and connect on social media.

I AM A VICTOR!

DEBBIE T. PROCTOR-CALDWELL

You Have 5 Minutes To Cry...
By Debbie T. Proctor-Caldwell

I have had a lot of mentors in my life, but no one beyond my parents shaped my life more than my paternal grandmother Louise, "Grandma Lucy." She had a saying when I was upset that stayed with me forever. No matter what the issue, she would tell me, "You've got five minutes to cry about it. After that, all you're doing is "stewing." I wondered to myself, "Wow, why is she rushing me? I am literally crying in front of her, and she is being so mean!" At the time, I didn't get it, and during the midst of life's problems, I didn't understand it. In time, I learned that it was more than just a saying, but a philosophy meant to be applied to the rest of my life.

While others in the 8th grade gym class were getting ready to change for their next class, I was told to stand by. I knew nothing good ever came from being held behind, and this would prove to be no different. Everyone was whispering all day at school about this random test, and it soon revealed that it would change my life forever.

Two fingers traced my spine as I bent over at my knees to then be told that I had Scoliosis of the spine. In my head, I was asking myself, what does that mean? What is this funny-sounding word, Scoliosis?! Fear of the unknown was written all over my face. Now that same whispering turned into a hush as I passed by my classmates. Everyone knew I was its next victim. My gym teacher broke the news to me in further detail by telling me that I needed to see a specialist, and if not, horrible things would happen to me in the future. Then my gym teacher sent me home with a letter to my parents. All I kept thinking about on my way home was what my gym teacher said last, "Without help, your body will turn against you." As if being a teenager and the only girl in a household with three older brothers and one younger brother wasn't hard enough, I now had to go through this. Deep down inside, I kept wondering, what if there isn't any real help? Will I die? Will my body turn against me enough to kill me?! What do I do now?

I later learned that Scoliosis of the spine was an abnormal curvature of the spine that causes a sideways curve of the spine in an "s" or "c" shape. If left untreated, it could lead to breathing and heart problems because the rib cage could slowly twist and crush my heart and/or prevent my lungs from expanding fully. Surgery back then was not an option for me. My parents were too afraid for me to have surgery to correct the curvature, thinking I would become paralyzed. There was not enough information available at the time to make my parents feel comfortable about me having surgery. Especially not for what they felt was an elective surgery for a disease they never heard of. So, they opted for a back brace for me.

The pain I experienced in my back prior to the diagnosis, I chucked up to what I saw on the tv show, "The Jefferson's." I thought that all I needed was a good back massage similar to what "George" did by walking on "Bentley's" bad back. But this condition led to three of my four years of high school being placed in a "Milwaukee" back brace, and the pain associated with this followed me into adulthood. This back brace made of steel was worn every day under my clothes like a corset but also seen outside my clothing along my neck area. It was extremely uncomfortable to wear, walk, sit, and even sleep in as required, but it became a part of my body. I could not participate in sports. I felt ostracized by my classmates and stared at in public. As if being a teenager was not already filled with insecurities, now it's multiplied by one hundred!

At sixteen, my doctor provided me with a note excusing me from a mandatory gym class requirement for high school graduation that stated that I was disabled. I was crushed! Disabled?! I thought to myself, "This medical condition isn't permanent! I can take the brace off! How can you write that I am disabled"?! I felt labeled. I demanded that the letter be rewritten to read "temporarily disabled" while wearing the back brace. This began the journey of me learning to overcome life's difficult moments for the rest of my life. But I learned that day… Never allow someone to place you in a box … EVER!

Upon graduation, I was no longer required to wear the back brace. I thought I was free. But in time, I realized that my back pain would be a part of me for the rest of my life. I did not know that this medical condition carried a stigma with it depending on who was across the other side of the table discussing it with me. It was as if my wearing the back brace as a teenager would be held against me like a criminal record.

When I was twenty-one years old, I became interested in law enforcement. I had applied to a local police department and had obtained a high score on my exam. I was ecstatic about my results. But once my background investigation into my medical history revealed that I had worn a back brace, I was no longer considered an eligible candidate for the next police recruit class.

I was about to give up on a law enforcement career before it even began based on this rejection. Why bother is what I thought? I'll just stay comfortable in my current "good government job." But I was twenty-one years old, intelligent, hyper, and bored. I visited "Grandma Lucy" and ended up crying on her shoulder and her telling me, "You've got five minutes to cry about it. After that, all you're doing is "stewing."

That "No" coupled with my Grandma Lucy's philosophy set a fire inside of me that still keeps me determined, focused, and persistent when there is something that I want to do or accomplish! When faced with rejection or failure, I remind myself of these two mottos:

1. No, does not mean no forever. It just means not right now.
2. Where there's a will, there's away. I just need to find it.

So, I dusted myself off, got out of my own way, accepted the fact that this back pain was a part of me and did not define me, and kept applying. Within that year, I was offered employment at two high profile police departments that were at the top of my list.

Fast forward 25 years later, I was now coming to a close in my career in law enforcement. I not only became a police officer; I rose through the ranks from being a new recruit/officer to Sergeant to Lieutenant. I went back to school and earned my Associates Degree in Science while working the midnight shift and later earned my bachelor's and master's Degrees from Johns Hopkins University in Baltimore, MD.

I became a VICTOR over my medical condition. I learned how to apply my Grandma Lucy's philosophy towards so many of life's disappointments, hurt, sorrow, and frustration to become a victor over my life! My Grandma Lucy was teaching me how to be strong and independent, which ultimately taught me how to develop instinct and problem solve. I learned that I could either allow this one incident and every incident afterward to rule my life by staying in neutral and crying, or I could cry for five minutes to let out my emotions and begin to solve the problem. Either way, it was not going to solve itself. Nowadays, I still cry when I get upset, but I use it as a stress-reliever! I do not stay parked in the "pity" parking lot with the same problem or issue. I wipe my tears and plan my strategy to solve the problem/issue(s). Below is a list that I use to continue to be a VICTOR, and you too can use to help yourself become one over your life when faced with tough decision(s) and or problem(s):

1. **Have your moment of self-pity.** Don't park yourself in the "pity" parking lot.
2. **Research the issue**; list pros & cons.

3. **Prioritize the items that need to be completed to accomplish the goal.** Take it step by step.
4. **Network with others**, seek advice, and join support groups familiar with your issue or problem.
5. **Pray/ meditate about it.**
6. **Give back.** Reach one, teach one, and teach more.

Always jump over the hurdles in life! Be a VICTOR!

BIO

Debbie Proctor-Caldwell is a Wife, Mother of two adult children and Stepmother to her bonus Son. She is from Southern Maryland but currently living in Washington D.C. In 2015, she retired as a police lieutenant from the United States Capitol Police in Washington D.C. with over 25 years of experience in law enforcement, investigations and public speaking and is now an aspiring author and an aspiring international motivational speaker.

Debbie is a child of God and attends the First Baptist Church of Glen Arden of Maryland. She earned her bachelor's degree and Master of Science in Management from Johns Hopkins University of Baltimore, Maryland.

Debbie is currently in the process of building her business that will serve to empower Women with leadership skills and the tools needed to create Generational Wealth.

Contact Info:
Email:Terenacspeaks@gmail.com
LinkedIn: Debbie Proctor-Caldwell, M.S.

TYKESHA REED

THE OVERACHIEVING PEOPLE-PLEASER
BY TYKESHA REED

I've always worked hard to please people, and not long ago, I began to wonder why. I thought back to my childhood, teenage years, and adulthood. I was curious about why I always felt the need to constantly set and accomplish goals? Why am I always planning? How did I become an overachiever? Why do I strive for perfection? Why do I cater to others even when it doesn't serve me? Why do I put others before myself? Like many of you, the pandemic of 2020 was the perfect time for me to reflect, journal, and heal from many of these toxic traits I found myself exhibiting. I grouped these traits as "overachieving" and "people-pleasing." I decided to take some life-changing steps and put in work to change myself for the better.

THE OVERACHIEVER

From the tender age of 14, I began working my first summer job. I wanted to purchase certain things for myself, so I worked in my church's daycare center because I enjoyed helping the children. I still remember how excited I was when I received my first paycheck. My heart was pounding extremely fast, and I had to catch my breath to talk because I was so happy to have earned my own money. There I was, looking at my first paycheck and planning how it would be spent. The satisfaction and exhilaration I experienced at that moment activated my journey of being an overachiever.

Over the next two summers, I started working not one, but two jobs. I was in high school and didn't need two jobs. However, I loved the fulfillment I felt after completing a goal, regardless of how difficult it was. While most teenagers were spending their weekends hanging out and having fun, I worked an early morning shift at McDonald's and a retail job during the weeknights. I realized that one job would not allow me to get what I wanted, so I worked two jobs. Sacrifice was no stranger to me, even as a teenager. I sometimes missed events and gatherings because I was working, but I never regretted it because I felt a sense of accomplishment and success.

You may think, what is wrong with being an overachiever? Some people believe that overachievers are smart, successful, and hard-working; many times, they are. However, overachievers strive for perfection and often have perfectionism, which is a disposition to regard anything short of perfection as unacceptable (Merriam-Webster). Unfortunately, I have to agree with the dictionary; we (overachievers) do strive for perfection. The problem is that perfectionism is about the fear of failure, which plays a part in being an overachiever.

I still cannot pinpoint where the need to be perfect came from. I can admit to the fear of failure, which is why every goal I've ever set, I have accomplished. The determination to not fail, combined with the fulfillment of completing a plan, gave me the drive to go above and beyond.

As an adult, I found myself always planning. My mind would work all day, trying to think of the next thing I needed to do. For example, I could have been watching a movie, and if it wasn't interesting, my mind would start thinking about all of the tasks I could have been doing instead of watching the movie. I would often think about ways I could be more productive instead of relaxing or enjoying the moment. I would always plan short and long-term goals with the intent of being in control and a step ahead. Some people that know me well believe that I am an outgoing and goal-oriented person with a type-A personality. They are correct. Others would say that I am a type-C personality, which is modest and patient, also correct. The differentiation is those that see me when I wear my entrepreneurial hat know that I am a leader and a go-getter that runs multiple organizations. They don't see me planning each step of my life, hating to fail at anything, and striving for perfection. The overachiever in me shows my type-A personality. Now, let's get back to the type-C personality that I mentioned.

THE PEOPLE PLEASER

People with type-C personality traits are calm, sensitive, passive, self-sacrificing people who tend to keep their emotions inside and mostly focus on others' feelings and thoughts, people-pleasers. The Merriam-Webster dictionary says a people pleaser has an emotional need to please others, often at the expense of their own needs or desires. Unfortunately, this was me. I had a bad habit of trying to please everyone, even when it cost me my peace of mind. I had to dig deep into this and figure out how I got there. I thought back to childhood. I was always taught to be kind to everyone and to respect my elders. I was a compassionate child who enjoyed making others happy, and I hated arguing and conflict. I would go out of my way to avoid conflict, even if it meant doing things, which I did not want to do. I believe it was the mindset of avoiding conflict regardless of how it made me feel that started me on the path at a young age of putting others before myself, people-pleasing.

I have always gone out of my way to help people. I sincerely enjoy helping, empowering, and mentoring others, but it wasn't until last year that I began to manage my time and take time for myself. For example, there are many times when I have been late for commitments because I was overbooking myself. Why, because I wanted to help everyone. Therefore, I filled all of my free time with tasks to help others, instead of allowing myself time to relax instead of rushing to my commitments; again, putting others before myself. There were also times when I went against my better judgment to avoid conflict.

As an adult, I cried, became frustrated and hurt that people would be so selfish and not reciprocate the same energy, effort, time, or compassion that I've overwhelmingly given to others. For as long as I can remember, I have given most of myself to others while leaving very little and, at times, NOTHING for myself. I am not one to ask for help, so most people would never know that I was burnt out. However, as a people-pleaser, I kept my hurt to myself and continued to press on and not burden anyone else.

After speaking with a friend about people-pleasing, she assured me that I would still be a kind and good person if I did not say "yes" to everything. I could still be compassionate and caring while not overbooking and putting myself first. She encouraged me to say no and to be ok with it. Self-care is a must, and now I understand and advocate for it.

My life is typically very busy and hectic. I thank God for aligning my life with lots of quietness to reflect on over the past year. This allowed me to transform my thinking, to stand up for myself, and to put myself first for once. I've also learned to say "no" instead of people-pleasing. This transformation allowed me to reflect on my purpose and dreams, which helped me to create one goal versus multiple, as I usually would. Last and most impactful was changing my mindset to excellence over perfection. Now, I am living out loud and intentionally surrounding myself with people that appreciate and support me for who I am authentically.

If you are experiencing the challenges that I mentioned in my story, I sincerely believe that you can overcome them, just as I have. Take the time weekly to practice the steps below until they become a habit. If you put in the work, you will be a VICTOR over your circumstances.

1. **Take the time to journal and process the negative traits that you want to change.** Ask yourself, where did these traits

originate, and do you own them? Release any traits that no longer serve you and replace them with positive behaviors.

2. **Feed your mind daily** with positive affirmations, books, and people.
3. **Practice Self-Care**; make yourself a priority.
4. **Say, "No."** Advocate for yourself; no one else will.
5. **Stay away from people that are negative or that have negative vibes.**
6. **FAIL FORWARD**; failure is a part of the process but keep going.

I believe in you and know that you can do this! This is a lifestyle change, so it will not be easy. However, I promise that you will see significant differences in your life after applying these steps. I wish you much success. Feel free to contact me for support, or if you have questions, I am here for you.

Be blessed!

BIO

Tykesha Reed is a motivational speaker and inspirational facilitator. Her passion drives her to empower women and girls to be their best selves. As a motivational speaker, Tykesha teaches women how to achieve their goals and lead with intention. She focuses on personal development, self-improvement, and self-care.

Tykesha is also an experienced Information Technology Trainer in higher education. For over 20 years, she has been a noteworthy leader in the information technology space. She has been honored with the Technology Rising Star Award from the Women of Color STEM Conference and IBM Corporation. Tykesha holds a Bachelor's degree from Coppin State University and a Master's degree from University of Maryland, Baltimore County. Tykesha is currently a doctoral student at Drexel University in Educational Leadership and

Management. Tykesha's goal is to be a blessing to whomever she comes in contact with and make a global impact on women worldwide.

Contact: theselfcareadvocate4u@gmail.com
Website: www.theselfcareadvocate4u.com
Instagram: TheSelfCareAdvocate4u

I AM A VICTOR!

JANISHA RICHARDSON

WHAT *IS* THIS C.P.A. THING ANYWAY?
BY JANISHA RICHARDSON

"I'm sorry, Sir; the car you reserved is not available. Can I interest you in an upgrade at no additional cost?"

Customer, "No, I want the car I reserved."

"Alright, Sir, I'm sorry for the delay. Let me see what I can do. Do you mind waiting a few minutes while I find a car for you?"

I hurried outside to see what cars are available. The car that the customer requested is here, but not clean. I am a Management Trainee at Enterprise Rental Car. It is 115-degrees outside in Fresno, California. I'm 23 years old, wearing heels, stockings, and a dress suit. The car that my customer reserved is dirty, and there is no one available to clean it. I proceeded to wash and vacuum the car.

This wasn't my first time getting a car ready for a customer, but at that moment, something clicked; I have a degree in accounting, and I worked hard for my degree. Why wasn't I using it? The truth is, once I graduated, I didn't want to work in accounting; I just wanted to graduate and start making money. On that hot sunny day, with sweat dripping down my face, I realized I appreciated my degree. I didn't have to be sweating in 115-degree heat, washing cars in a dress suit. Instead, I could be sitting in an air-conditioned office crunching numbers.

Over the next few months, I started looking for a job in accounting. I went on several interviews but never received a job offer. During my search, I found H & R Block offered a Tax Preparer class. Upon completion, you could work for them during tax season. I took the class, passed the test, and became a Tax Preparer. I continued to work from 7 am - 7 pm at Enterprise and worked at H & R Block from 7:30 pm - 11 pm on the weekdays and 8 am - 5 pm on the weekends. During my four months working in the tax industry, I developed a love for preparing tax returns. My first tax season was busy, challenging, and stressful, but I learned so much and enjoyed every minute of it. After the tax season ended, I knew I didn't want to continue working at Enterprise.

While talking with my younger sister, Jania, I shared my struggles of finding a job in accounting.

She said, "You should move to Washington, D.C. There are a lot of firms that will hire African-Americans with business degrees out here."

To give you some personal background, after high school, I received a track scholarship to attend California State University, Fresno. There I earned my Bachelor of Science Degree in Business Administration and Accounting. My sister, on the other hand, was on a different mission. As soon as she graduated high school, she moved across the country to attend Howard University, a Historically Black College. During her undergraduate years, I visited D.C. as often as I could. I saw Prince in concert, and I witnessed my sister joining the Alpha Kappa Alpha Sorority, Howard's Homecoming, and of course, her graduation from Howard University. Moving to D.C. sounded like a great opportunity. At the time, my sister was in her second year at Howard Law School and wasn't sure if she was going to stay in D.C. or move back to California after graduation. I prayed for guidance, and in 1998 made a move to Washington, D.C.

Coming from Fresno and moving to Chocolate City at 26 years old was shocking. One of the main differences was in D.C., everyone asked, "Where did you attend college?" The first question in California

I AM A VICTOR!

was, "How many kids do you have?" Right then, I knew I was on a different playing field. I was hired as a Junior Accountant at an African-American-owned Certified Public Accountant firm within my first week. Antony Smith, the company owner, was extremely persistent and supportive of me obtaining my C.P.A. license. In 1998, everyone I met was in their mid-twenties, had a high-paying job in the private or government sector, had/or was working on their Master's Degree, was a homeowner, or was about to purchase a house. I felt in order for me to fit into my new surroundings, I had to become Janisha Richardson, C.P.A. I became very serious about studying and passing the exam.

When I would meet people, I would often tell them that I was studying to take the C.P.A. exam. The C.P.A. became the focus of my conversation. Although, I assumed everyone knew what C.P.A. stood for, people would often ask, "What is this C.P.A. thing anyway?" I would explain that C.P.A. stands for Certified Public Accountant, and the exam was taken over two days, covering four sections of accounting. To pass, you needed a minimum score of 75. The exam was only offered twice a year, during the first week in May and November. The more I worked and met other professionals, the more I knew passing the exam and having those three letters behind my name would validate me professionally.

In May 2004, I passed three of the four sections after five years of significant sacrifice. I was almost to the finish line. My final exam, in November 2004 would be the last paper exam. In 2005, the C.P.A. exam was converting to a computerized format. Mind you, I had been taking the paper exam for the previous five years. Yes, I had taken the exam non-stop for five years. My life was centered around May and November every year. I allowed those three letters to control my life, define my knowledge, and define me. Scoring a 75 in November was my last chance to pass the paper exam. Over the next five months, I studied, took the exam, and scored a 72... three points from passing. Three points from being called Janisha Richardson, C.P.A... 3 points! I was sick, angry, and defeated. I went so far as to submit my exam results to be reexamined. A month later, Maryland responded with no change in my score. I was devasted again. I cried, I threw up, I asked God WHY? I was in a very dark place. But I couldn't stay there. I had to pass the last section by November 2005. If I didn't, I would lose the three sections that I had already passed.

The computerized C.P.A. exam was ridiculous! The whole format changed from the paper exam. I took it twice, and both times failed. I was shattered; I had spent countless hours and thousands of dollars over the last six years taking this exam. After losing all of my credits to become a C.P.A., I decided to take a break from taking the exam and focused on counting my blessings. While studying for the exam, I had been hired by a top C.P.A. firm in 2004. I had also started an accounting and tax business. During this break, I focused on growing my business and became involved in my community. One day, a friend asked me to run for the Advisory Neighborhood Commission (ANC) position in Ward 1A. I had no idea what that was, but he said my community needed me and I should run. I gathered the required signatures, and in 2004, I become an elected official in Washington, D.C. During my term, I represented 3,000 constituents and served as ANC 1A Treasurer for four years.

Having those three letters behind my name didn't seem as important. Don't get me wrong, I still wanted it very badly, but I no longer needed it to define me. It took 20 years and a lot of work, but I finally realized that I didn't need those three letters to validate who I am. I had the experience. I had validation from my community, clients, peers, and most importantly, myself. I finally recognized my worth. I invested in myself by reshifting my energy to my family, community, church, self-care, and travel. Once I reshifted my strength, I become a victor over self-doubt and self-pity.

Without those three letters, I have become a real estate entrepreneur, community activist, Co-Founder of Richardson & Moore, LLC, and

I AM A VICTOR!

Positive Business Credit Solutions, LLC. I finally realized that I didn't need those three letters to validate my knowledge. I was finally living in my purpose as an entrepreneur, networker, connector, and motivator.

In closing, I may not have those letters behind my name, but I am self-validated. My pursuit of obtaining my C.P.A. license is not closed. I'm just pursuing my passions and living in my purpose. My pursuit for obtaining my C.P.A. continues, but now on my terms.

Things I did to become a Victor:

- Self-care "Staycations"
- Journaling: List 1-year and 5-year goals. Write down your fears-let go and let God
- Join professional organization(s)
- Network:-Be intentional with where you go and who you want to meet
- Spiritual care:-God as my foundation

BIO

Janisha Richardson, a native of Clovis, California, holds a Bachelor of Science Degree in Business Administration and Accounting from California State University, Fresno. An avid sports enthusiast, Janisha competed as a collegiate track athlete and started her very first entrepreneurial venture as an event planner, organizing events centered around college students. In 2003, Janisha co-founded Richardson & Moore, LLC, an accounting and tax services company in Washington, D.C. Her experience as a business advisor, working with new entrepreneurs to grow their business, gave her unique insight into the challenges they encountered because of limited access to capital. It was a desire to address this problem that motivated her to start Positive Business Credit Solutions, LLC in 2019. Janisha is passionate about financial literacy and economic empowerment in underserved communities. Janisha enjoys, traveling, sports, and spending time with family.

Website: www.pbcs-llc.com
IG: pbcsllc
Email: jrich@pbcs-llc.com

I AM A VICTOR!

SELENA ROBINSON

THE SURPRISE VISIT
BY SELENA ROBINSON

There is a quote by Woody Allen that says, "If you want to make God laugh, tell him about your plans. Plans were precisely what I was thinking about as we were ending the year 2019 and entering the year 2020.

Two-thousand-nineteen was an extremely challenging year for me, particularly the latter part of the year, I broke my ankle, then immediately after healing from the injury, I developed influenza. Both instances required me to remain still, something that was unfamiliar.

So, to say I was ready for a new year was an understatement. The new year, for me, symbolized a reflection of the past and a resolve of what I could do better. I recall New Year's Eve when I counted down to the new year: five, four, three, two, one... Happy New Year. I was eager to celebrate I had made it through 365 days; the time had come for me to raise my glass and toast to another year of survival. In the days ahead, I would prepare to have some sort of control over my upcoming year. I began to do what many of us do - visualize what I wanted my new year to resemble. I was so happy and ready to execute my plans. Again, if you missed that, I was prepared to execute MY plans, not God's Plan.

Even though I knew the year could be unpredictable, I never imagined three days into the new year, something would sound the alarm and change my life forever. It all began one night while I was lying in bed alone; I was experiencing a bad headache, my left eye was hurting, and it felt inflamed. The symptoms were a bit unusual as the pain was in my temples. The pain was so bad that merely touching my temples made me want to scream. I could not stand the light on in the room, and sharp pains came from my left eye. I lay there thinking, should I just stick the pain out and see if I felt better in the morning. But something said, *Selena, get up and drive yourself to the hospital.* So, I decided to drive to the hospital to put my mind at ease. You see, I just thought I would be offered some migraine medicine and sent on my merry way. I got to the hospital and was assisted by a Physician Assistant. They ran several tests, one crucial test being a CAT scan (computerized axial tomography). When the doctor came back in the room to give me my test results, he began with the CAT scan, and reported the CAT scan came back normal. I was so relieved, but shortly after, he said, "I do have some concerns about your blood test." He told me my Sed Rate (erythrocyte sedimentation rate, also known as ESR) helps detect inflammation in the body. He informed me that the standard SED rate for a woman is generally 0 to 22; he indicated my rate was a 90. He also explained a disease caused the pain in my temples and eyes, which affected the blood vessels, called arteries, in my head. But as if that was not the bad news, he dropped the real bomb: he said that it could cause vision loss, and I needed to see several specialists immediately as I could go blind in an instant. You can imagine he had my attention by this point. I sat straight up, completely shocked by what the doctor said my eyesight had to be saved. He gave me some medicine, which I call the angel/devil drug (prednisone), which should preserve my eyesight in the interim. He also said I would require surgery on my temples to diagnose my condition further, which I had on July 17, 2020. After hearing all this, I was utterly overwhelmed. I left the hospital devastated, thinking I could lose my eyesight and be disabled.

I would later visit many specialists, including my primary physician, who I trust and admire; she would confirm the diagnosis and share with me that my illness would fall under the category of CHRONIC ILLNESS DISEASE. I had no idea chronic diseases affected approximately 133 million Americans, and I was instantly counted in that number. She explained that my lifestyle would change and removed me from the workforce for eight weeks. I remember that day so vividly; I left the office and sat outside in my car for two hours wailing. Once I finally got myself together, I turned on the ignition, and the song that was playing was "Patiently Praising," by Fred Jerkins." The words resonated in my heart.

Got some bad news from the physician.
My heart started pounding as I listened.
To what was said,
Cause in my head, I never thought it could happen to me.

That was just a cliff note of the song, but it prompted me to let me know I was in for another encounter with my familiar friend named perseverance. You see, I had just written a chapter in a book called the Power of Perseverance about tips on how to persevere; my faith would be tested once again, but this time the stakes were much higher, and I felt weaker. God spoke to me and said it's good to deliver, but you have to live it. It was at that point that Ephesians 6:10-18 (KJV) came to mind. Finally, my brethren, be strong in the Lord and in the power of his might. Put on the whole armor of God, that ye may be able to stand against the wiles of the devil.

My heart was aching, and the disappointment was grand. I was experiencing trauma. I felt like I had broken the integrity of my health. Disappointments in life were no stranger to me as they are inevitable, but what I did know was misery was OPTIONAL. I had to pray, but I had to have a plan for how I was going to make it out of the valley. I had to transform from dark to light. The transformation would require me to release all the emotions I was feeling inside to begin to accept the diagnosis. I knew I had to change my perspective and my narrative to grace my new self. To accomplish this, I had to do some real centering and make a shift, so this would not become my new identity. I am leaning in to tell my story because it's me today, but it could be you tomorrow. In a matter of minutes, something can alter your whole life.

So, in exchange for my vulnerability, I want you to pledge to do the following if you find yourself in a similar situation.

- Never underestimate your instincts
- Take back your time because life is a gift, and every moment counts
- Always remember your health is truly your wealth
- As Richard Carlson so elegantly put it, "Don't Sweat the Small Stuff."
- Cherish the ability to SEE

But most importantly, I need you to PUSH through.

P- Pivot and Posture yourself to think about the lessons and the blessings behind every situation.

U-Understand that joy does come in the morning. Learn to live with the uncertainty of life as we have no control.

S- Gather your support system. Understand that support looks different for each individual. Manage your expectations of others and know that you are stronger than you think you are.

H- Harvest the strength to ask for help, put your pride and ego aside. Asking for help is a strength, not a weakness.

As a bonus, I share with you an important lesson I have learned. And is that several people are walking around with invisible illnesses. The worst part of this journey was some of my family and friends not understanding the magnitude of what I was going through. The hardest thing for me to hear was Silence from others.

I AM A VICTOR!

I want to let you know out of this experience, my superpower was ignited, my vision. I realized my assignment from God is essential. I understand if my plan is not available anymore, and I am presented with option B, I am still rich with gratitude. My goal is to strive to take aligned action to receive what I want to manifest in my life. The irony this moment has emphasized to me is that you don't have to see to take the next step.

In conclusion, as I Rewind, Replay, and Reflect on this occurrence, I am confident of the discernment I am not a victim. I am a VICTOR. Currently, I am striving to get my illness under control while claiming healing. Special thanks to my support tribe as they help me manage stress and emotions. More importantly, I am happy for the surprise visit that saved my sight.

BIO
Selena Robinson is an Amazon Best Seller Co-Author of the Power of Perseverance, Coach, and Motivational Speaker. She has a sweet spot for inspiring others to "Create memories and strengthen relationships." She is a networking strategist and a picture taking queen who enjoys shopping, and event planning. She is a champion of positivity and inclusivity and a lifetime member of Alpha Kappa Alpha Sorority Inc. In her professional role she serves as a contracting officer for the Federal Government in Frederick Maryland. She earned a M.A, in Administration and Supervision with a concentration in Training, and B.A in Communications Studies from Montclair State University in NJ.

One of her greatest accomplishments is her daughter Alaya Mone Robinson.

Find out more about Selena at:
Facebook. @NikkouChappelRobinson
Instagram: @Nikkouturns50
Clubhouse: @Nikkouselena68

DIMITRIA R. SCOTT

I CHOOSE ME
BY DIMITRIA R. SCOTT

"The worst wounds, the deadliest of them, aren't the ones seen on the outside."
Sherrilyn Kenyon

Anna was a talented, calm, and closely aligned thirteen-year-old. She lived in Steffisburg, Switzerland, in the 1880s with a selfish father and a sick mother. Anna grasped at straws from that innocent age because of her parent's negligence. Just like any growing child, Anna nurtured the beautiful dreams sprouting from her fertile heart.

Unfortunately, the cranky old man believed it was better to marry his daughter out than to help her nurture her dreams. And her sickly mother was too weak to defend her. Left with no choice, Anna got married to a man she loathed at thirteen and had six kids for him.

Marrying such a Hippo for a husband turned the plumpy Anna into a withered leaf with no spine to reflect her beauty and elegance. She walked through life with her head bowed like a lonesome George. Even though she tried to match the epitome of an excellent mother and the idea of an awesome wife— as her mother had advised, she was yet lost in the midst of nowhere.

She was crushed and sapped of life by marriage. She was too young to start a family, and the constant reminder that she had to forgo her dreams drowned her joy and happiness in the ocean of pity. Her naggy husband became obnoxious, and she had to pretend to be fine for her kids and herself.

THE DISCONNECT

Like Anna, you must realize that the journey through life will be marked by valleys of pains and trauma and mountains of victory. Experiences like the death of a loved one, sickness, failure, depression, or abuses are unpalatable experiences that you often have no control over.

Have you ever felt so emotionally empty and dissatisfied? Feeling alone even when you are among a group of people? I have been there. I was once trapped in the mud of my past experiences. I allowed my past dirge-moments to get into the beautiful symphony of my present realities.

Yes! I felt lost, and sometimes, despised. I disengaged from the rest of the world. And started to live in my lonely shell of pain. Everything became blurry and gloomy like a sky without the smile of the sun. But then, something happened that turned my pains into power— I choose me!

Do you know the Bible story of Job and the huge blow of trauma life dealt him? Job's season was a living instance of undergoing extreme agony, rejection, neglect, and pain. He felt so tortured that he couldn't help but complain. The fullness of his pains spilled out his mouth in Job 10:1(KJV). He said, "My soul is weary of my life; I will leave my complaint upon myself; I will speak in the bitterness of my soul." This was how fed up Job was. Can you relate to Job's dilemma?

JOURNEYING BACK TO ME.

"Though I fall, I will rise again."
Micah 7:8

I AM A VICTOR!

While in-depth of pity and depression, I had what I call a prodigal-son moment. It was as though the thick veil of self-pity and low self-esteem fell off my heart. My mind was awakened to the endless world of possibilities within me. Just like the prodigal son, I decided not to allow my circumstance to define who I am. I came to myself!

The truth is self-discovery is a critical phase that only you can decide to undergo. This stage is so significant and constructive when you decide to start it. No matter how greasy it might seem at first, the path to self-discovery is a honeycomb of emancipation and fulfillment.

How do you let go of those past aches and traumas? How will you be able to recall the past and smile? Well, you must discover yourself. You must choose yourself over your windy past. Rid yourself of the chains of tears you struggle with. Accept that you've had some pretty bad times and accept that it's time to burst free of living in the hurts of life. Realize that the future's been waiting for you for so long! Know that it's time to step into the light. Have that confidence in yourself.

Moreover, until you accept your faults and acknowledge you are human to have committed them, you'd never be able to develop into a better version of yourself. See the good in you. Yes, you had an ugly past, but never let your past build a war against your glorious future and destiny!

From God's standpoint, you're an amazing individual. Even God concedes this in Genesis 2:31," And God saw everything He has made, and behold it was very good." Did you see that? These creatures of God include you. Yes, you! In fact, you're the most special of them all. God did something He never did for other creatures for you- He made you in His perfect image! Can you imagine that? You're one image as God! That is interesting and endearing, isn't it? If you don't celebrate anything about yourself, celebrate this truth. Love who you are as a special and highly-favored creature of the Lord.

Until you start seeing the good in you and start celebrating them, life's gonna remain the same. Andy Warhol once said, "They said that time changes things, but you have to change them yourself." See that? Nothing might ever change if you don't appreciate yourself. No matter how hard it seems, remember you can do all things through Christ, which strengthens you. Philippians 4:13.

Also, yearn for the Lord. Lamentations 3:25 proclaims," The Lord is good to those who wait for Him, for those who seek Him." Seeking the Lord means you're rediscovering yourself in Him. And He will help you overcome all that might want to discourage your quest. The Holy Spirit will guide you through the new path you want to walk. Jeremiah 30:17 assures you of this, "For I will restore health unto thee, and I will heal thee of thy wounds, saith the Lord; because they called thee an Outcast, saying, this is Zion, whom no man seeketh after."

"I Choose Me"

I was a masterpiece, created by The Master's hands, and the world was a canvas for me,

But the choices of man made me not believe, and God's Jeremiah 29:11 plan

halted because of wounds that no eye could see.

Planted deep internally, the trauma that was stained affected me,

opening the door for self-inflicted pain and overwhelming doubt,

To others, I appeared to be alive and free, but mentally, I was waist-deep in quicksand

with no idea or drive to get out.

Depression and anxiety were my shackles, attached to my mind. How was I to ever break free?

Then that's when I heard a still sweet voice whisper, 'I created you in the image of Me.'

I AM A VICTOR!

The One Who spoke the words that I heard had to have known it was exactly what I would need,

Because I found enough strength to dig in the darkness, I was in, to find my mustard seed.

Holding on to it tight, the light illuminated bright, revealing the value I began to see in me,

I then became deliberate about life, understanding God's plan, fully appreciating intentionality.

I began chasing purpose instead of paper; taking in every experience to teach others the lessons I've

learned,

I omitted negativity completely to receive the joy that my spirit has always yearned!

The growth of my intellect and wisdom from reading daily is a right I've truly earned.

Yielding to the process has caused the shackles to open, the links have broken, and I am loosed and

free,

I've got VICTORY, now standing upright and poise, I've made the choice that I… CHOOSE… ME!!!

You can also have VICTORY if you

V- VALUE WHO YOU ARE

I– be INTENTIONAL

C– COMMIT TO CHANGE

T– TELL YOUR TRUTH

O– OMIT NEGATIVITY

R– READ AND EDCUATE YOURSELF DAILY & RESIST BEING A PEOPLE PLEASER

Y– YIELD TO THE PROCESS

Ultimately, know that only you can make a difference in your life. If there's something you don't like, change it. Shed the tattered materials of your hurts and dejection, make that trip back to the beautiful you, and you'll be victorious at the end. The Lord wants this for you. Jeremiah 29:11 says," For I know the thoughts that I think toward you, saith the Lord, thoughts of peace, and not of evil, to give you an expected end.

Therefore, you are enough! You are a Victor!

BIO

Minister, Mentor, Motivator

Dimitria is dedicated to ministering, mentoring, and motivating teen moms, young women and those who may feel hopeless and like an outcast. She is the founder of Real Sister, Victorious Partners, a community of women committed to growing together in life's journey. Her goal is to expand her non-profit, Motivating Teen Mom's Academy, a program to help teen moms overcome the challenges they face in this role. Transitional homing with a school and daycare facility is provided, where these teens will live, learn, and raise their children in a safe environment.

Facebook is Dimitria R Scott
Instagram is MrsDRScott
Email mrsdrscott@gmail.com

I AM A VICTOR!

DR. MARY SEGARS

THE POWER OF MY VOICE!
BY DR. MARY SEGARS

"He who refused to stoop, who cannot be bribed by the promise of success or the fear of failure – who walks the highway of the right, and in disaster stands erects, is the only victor."
Robert Green Ingersoll

When you know, like you know your name, that your voice and message are to be heard worldwide, so you keep that in the front of your mind, and so does the enemy who wants to steal your voice!

I can tell you since I was a young girl, my Mom knew that I could use my voice to express myself clearly. In her wisdom, she made sure that I utilized that gift, so I was in church's performance and other activities to speak my truth, and my voice was heard!

Fast forward; my life has afforded me to utilize my voice to speak not only my truth but to impart the gospel truth to the lost and the saints of God. I was ordained and licensed as a minister, and I spoke with authority and power. I didn't take that precious gift God has given me for granted, but I guarded it in my heart. In my workplace, I thrived in Human Resources and exceeded in the corporate environment where I flourished in Executive Communications, and I assisted in preparing speeches for executives. There again, I valued written and the spoken communication in the workplace. Before I took an early retirement from corporate, I enjoyed training executives for Leadership Development. I was drawn to Toastmasters to sharpen my speaking techniques and won many accolades for my speaking abilities. I've conducted seminars where I shared with hundreds of people the importance of knowing your purpose. I taught clients about their motivation traits and how to live a fulfilled life. I was on non-profit boards and voiced my expertise to help the non-profit organizations strengthen their presence in the community. Life was good!

As life happens to everyone, it happened to me. I've always had excellent annual health exams, and I focused on having a workout regimen. I had the pleasure of teaching Jazzercise at my church. Several times I had to retake my mammograms due to suspicious results, but everything turned out okay. I've enjoyed praying for others who encountered bad test results, and I believed for complete healing and recovery for them. I gave them scriptures to support their faith regarding healing.

In 2013, my business flourished, and my clientele increased as my referral business was awesome! I remember it was a summer day in July 2013, and I had a very meaningful and successful coaching session with my client. After our meeting, I left my office and encouraged my client to continue to make progress, as she was achieving her goals and making strides in her leadership development. You can imagine how I felt, like a proud parent recognizing your child's growth and success. I smiled, getting into my car, and my drive home was only a 15-minute drive. I left feeling satisfied that I'm doing what I was destined to do. While stopped at a red light, I listened to my gospel music on the radio, and I was singing along, waiting for the light to change to green, suddenly, a car came hurtling into my car head-on! Everything seemed like it was in slow motion. I could only call out to Jesus! The impact pushed my car back, and my glasses went flying in the air, landing on the floor. My neck jerked back and forward quickly, and thanks for my seat belt, which kept me secure. The steering wheel airbag discharged and thrust in my face and chest. I thought I was dreaming as I have never been in an accident before in all my years of driving!

I AM A VICTOR!

I slowly got out of my car dazed and confused. I couldn't talk at all. I glanced at my car, and the front end was totally smashed in, and the engine was smoking. The person who hit me was a young lady learning to drive. Her uncle, who was in the passenger seat, came out, and he had one arm, was teaching her how to drive and make turns. I was thinking to myself I was at the wrong place at the wrong time, but in actuality, I really was at the right place at the right time, and I'll explain why I say that later.

I was taken to the hospital via an ambulance, and the EMT worker put a neck brace on me to transport me to the emergency room. They took so many x-rays and informed me and my family that I didn't break any bones but to follow up with my personal doctor in a few days. I was released, and my thoughts were all over the place. The enemy was trying to take me out, but he didn't succeed! I knew that the Lord had yet even more for me to do for Him by the Power of My Voice! I won't shut-up, devil. What I have to say will be heard all over the world!

I can honestly say I'm thankful for the accident because it was revealed that I had Stage 2 Thyroid Cancer and the x-rays uncovered the one-inch nodule on my thyroid. I never had any symptoms like hard to swallow, etc., but I realized that the Lord needed to get my attention so this matter can be taken care of as I had to speak my truth. What I have to say by using my Voice was something that the world needed to hear by my voice! Initially, I would get upset when people would say something about my voice, but I didn't accept what others said, only what God told me – Your voice will be heard! I knew I was on assignment to use my Voice to change others' lives and make an impact.

Yes, my voice is deeper since my surgery, but I will magnify my voice to speak from my heart and let people know you can overcome all things and be a Victor! I refuse to be a victim because I am a Victor. In 2019, I was honored to be one of the keynote speakers at the Women's

Empowerment and Leadership Conference in Bangkok, Thailand. I spoke with authority and impact to the audience. I've authored two books, "Power Talk begins with Power Thoughts," explaining the importance of self-talk to victory; my other book, "Wake up the Leader within You." In 2020, I attended a Women's Economic Forum in Cairo, Egypt, and spoke and used my voice, which was heard worldwide. I've come to love the Power of My Voice because I know what I have to say will change lives, impact, and influence many. I am a Victor, and I know the Power of My Voice. What about you? You need to know you too can have Power in Your Voice!

BIO

Dr. Mary Segars is the Founder and CEO of Segars Consulting Group (SCG). SCG is committed to providing entrepreneurs and businesswomen the needed tools to be the best leaders in corporate and personal environments. She is a certified John Maxwell Speaker, Trainer and Coach. She has published two best-selling books; "Power Talk begins with Power Thought," and "Wake up the Leader within You."

Dr. Segars conducts seminars, training sessions on Leadership Competencies and Development, Personal Growth and Development, Life Mapping for Success, and Motivational Assessment to name a few. In addition, Dr. Segars is an international keynote speaker where she spoke at Women's Leadership Forum in Bangkok, Thailand in 2019 and at the Women Economy Forum (WEF) in Cairo, Egypt in 2020. Mary has been a virtual speaker at WEF Bangalore 2020 – Digital Summit since Covid-19.

Dr. Segars had been named to the Professional Women Network International Advisory Board for 2017-2018.

I AM A VICTOR!

TASHAYA J. SINGLETON

I AM A VICTOR!

VICTORY BEGINS WITH A DECISION
BY TASHAYA J. SINGLETON

Many of us go to work every day to a job that, frankly, we don't like. According to a Gallup poll, only 15% of us are actively engaged at work. And most of us do not leave our jobs because of the responsibilities called bills. We are either too dependent on direct deposit or filled with fear. Fear that if we leave our job, we may not get another one that is equal or better, or if we start a business, it will fail because of the statistics we hear about all the time. For most of us, the underlying, real reason is a lack of belief in ourselves.

I know because I used to be in the global group of the 85% of people that don't like their job but wouldn't leave. I stayed at a job that I didn't like, and it wreaked havoc on my health. But of course, like most of us, I didn't learn my lesson the first time. I did this not once, not twice, but three times.

I started working at an international bank and thought this was the job that I would stay at for 20 years and retire from, with all the opportunities they had. You could move around and work in different departments, and of course, the possibilities for advancement were endless, given the bank's size. I was a good employee and got along with my supervisors, Sherry and Randy. I was selected for special projects and worked in nine different departments of the bank under their supervision. Sherry left the bank to pursue another career, and Randy moved to a different department, and I got two new supervisors. I applied for Randy's position and was pulled into a conference room by a manager, Melody, and told that I wasn't qualified for the position

270

and needed more experience. Another person, Kim, who was friends with this manager, and Yvonne, a Vice President at the bank, was given the assistant supervisor position. I was constantly pulled from my desk to complete tasks that an assistant supervisor was required to do, that Kim didn't know how to do. So, here I was doing my job, and Kim's, the assistant supervisor, that was given the job that I was told by the manager Melody, that I didn't get because of lack of experience. To add insult to injury, I was no longer allowed to work on special projects because Melody felt I was doing too much and just needed to work in my department. Yvonne, a Vice President in my department, and the manager Melody, who was also good friends with Yvonne, called me in the office for my annual review. They told me that although I have perfect customer satisfaction scores, I spend entirely too much time with a customer, so I would not be eligible for my raise for another six months. So, I requested a review of my qualifications for the assistant supervisor position and my raise. It didn't take long for me to get written up for things, even though I could prove they didn't happen by showing pages from the logbook. I was being reprimanded for not being at my desk because I was helping a new employee. Then, I was reprimanded for not being a team player because I didn't leave my desk to help new employees. Soon, I started having migraines regularly. My doctor and I tried to figure out what was causing these migraines.

Doctor Ciccone ordered all sorts of tests on me, and they all came back negative. He was extremely concerned because I went from barely seeing him twice a year to being in his office frequently. Dr. Ciccone asked me to keep a journal and write down everything that was going on before the migraines happened. After a few weeks, Dr. Ciccone told me that I needed to quit my job because it was causing my migraines. I thought he was crazy!

My migraines got worse and worse. He told me to quit my job a second time. The third time he told me to quit my job, I told him I couldn't because I have rent and a car note payment. He said, "if you want to live, you'll quit your job." Guess what, I quit my job, and my migraines went away.

I was helping a friend with his insurance, and he said, why aren't you doing this for a living because you're passionate about it and really know what you're doing. So, I started working as an insurance agent, commission only, but I wasn't making enough to cover the bills, and I got another job at a health insurance company as a claim's representative. I planned to work a full-time job and work part-time in the insurance business until I was financially able to quit my job and do insurance full time.

One day, as I was leaving to attend a conference, with approved unpaid time off, my manager, Victoria, said, "I feel that if a person can take unpaid time off, they don't need a job." When I returned, the environment was hostile, similar to the bank, my migraines came back, and Dr. Ciccone told me to quit my job again. I said, "I have a mortgage and a car payment; I can't quit my job." And I decided to tough it out because I would have enough money saved to go full time in the insurance business in a few months. So, I listened to motivational messages, prayed, and distance myself as much as possible from my manager and department coworkers.

Coworkers complained daily about the job, other coworkers, and our manager. At lunchtime, I would sit in the cafeteria, in an area away from my department, and I realized employees in every department had the same complaints. So, I decided to eat lunch in my car while listening to motivational messages. I rushed to my car, at 5:00 PM daily, to turn on a motivational message to regain my sanity.

One morning, I pulled into the parking garage; I sat in my car and just cried and cried because I didn't want to go into work and couldn't believe the financial position I was in. Of course, I got another migraine while sitting there crying. I called in sick, went straight to my doctor's office for an emergency appointment, and Dr. Ciccone told me again to quit my job. And, this time, I did. I didn't care if I lost everything and became homeless; I wasn't going to work there ever again.

Of course, when money got tight, because I hadn't learned my lesson, I got another job at a large corporation. Within two months, I got a migraine that was so painful that I had to get a shot in the butt for the pain to go away. I quit that job immediately. That's when I decided to take control of my personal financial economy and life no matter what.

Assessing my situation and accepting what was, not seeing it as worse or better than it really was. I decided that if money got tight, I would take a job, short term, that improved my skills to make me a better insurance professional. Then, to take control of my mind to ensure my success, I began reading motivational books and listening to motivational messages daily. Finally, I took control of my environment, eliminating and distancing myself from the well-meaning but unsupportive people in my life.

Diving headfirst into the insurance and financial services industry, I achieved my definition of success with determination and good work ethics. I am an author, podcast host, premier industry trainer, and the founder of TJS Financial Solutions, LLC. Every day I wake up, I'm passionate about helping women take control of their personal financial economy and life.

Even though there have been many ups and downs along my journey, I wouldn't trade it for a minute because I've learned and have grown more resilient from my failures than my successes. I have shared my story to inspire you to believe in yourself, step out on faith, and remind you that you can take control of your personal financial economy and life to create something better than you could ever imagine.

I AM A VICTOR!

"The greatest reward comes when you give of yourself. It's about bettering the lives of others, being part of something bigger than yourself, and making a positive difference."
Nick Vujicic, Motivational Speaker

BIO

Tashaya Singleton is a Certified Risk Manager and founder of TJS Financial Solutions. She has more than a decade of experience in training and the financial services industry. She is dedicated to helping women take control of their personal economy and life

Tashaya, also, hosts "The Secrets Of Earning Money Show" podcast, which was inspired by her book "The Secrets of Earning Money: How You Can Get $300 - $1,500 Within 30-Days!". And is the author of the upcoming book "From $0.00 (Zero) to Financial $tability".

You can connect with her by visiting her website http://www.TJSFinancialSoulitions.com or www.TashaSingleton.com on LinkedIn

DR. PAMELA W. SMITH

TRIED IN THE FIRE BUT BLESSED THROUGH THE TEST!
BY DR. PAMELA W. SMITH

Dear friends, don't be surprised about the fiery trials that have come among you to test you. These are not strange happenings.
1 Peter 4:12

Confusion, embarrassment, and disbelief were just some of the emotions I felt one Sunday afternoon as my husband burst into his pastor's study, grabbed my hand, whisked me down the stairs to get our two young daughters, then fled the scene after being confronted by church members. What had just happened? Why was my heart beating so fast, and why were my footsteps feeling like I was running for my life but going nowhere? Surely, this chaotic experience I was having would not be my reality once someone shook me and woke me up from my sleep. But what seemed like a dream of being the First Lady of a thriving church turned out to be a nightmare when I heard those three words I never imagined a pastor, let alone my husband would say to me—"I was fired!"

While I never thought of myself as the perfect First Lady, having this position stripped from me was eye-opening. I felt the immediate impact of the fiery darts being hurled at me through gossip, rumors, and insults by church members. Why was this happening to me? After all, I was the devoted First Lady who lovingly served alongside my husband and faithfully gave my heart to parishioners. I was the First Lady who led the women's ministry, taught Sunday school, and said 'yes' to everyone and everything. I was the First Lady who strived to go beyond the stereotypes of walking in the shadow of my husband's ministry, raising "perfect" preachers' kids, and fulfilling parishioners' unrealistic expectations. As a pastor's wife, I typically had to deal with private matters in a public setting, so how would I make it through this ordeal? As the consequences of church conflict kept adversely impacting my family and me, my husband needed me to walk beside him while being tested in the fire.

When I began to face the heart-wrenching affliction of church hurt, I was left suffering in silence in the pews. After living through years of suppressing people's bold-faced lies and deception, I was left feeling battered, broken, and bruised by people who knew me well and by others who did not know me at all. Instead of donning a beautiful First Lady church hat, I chose to put on my L.I.D. (Loneliness, Isolation, and Despair). How I longed for someone, perhaps other pastors' wives, who knew what it was like to walk in my shoes, to take me under their wings. I desired to be in authentic and trustworthy relationships where I could confidentially share my pain with other first ladies who had also seen the good, the bad, and the ugly side of clergy marriage, ministry, and more. That desire would not be fulfilled soon enough; instead, as time went on, I attended other churches and harbored bitterness in my heart while wearing my mask, muting my voice, and fighting back the tears that were overflowing inside me. The overwhelming turbulence of church hurt had challenged my faith and rocked my world.

After being evicted from the church parsonage and disgraced in the community, my family set out to rebuild our lives in Charlotte, North Carolina. I prayed that my husband would pastor again, but God repeatedly said, 'wait.' While the awful memories of the church conflict impacted my life in ways that steered me down a gloomy and lonely path, my heart was overjoyed when God finally after 18 years, called my husband to pastor another church. I felt so blessed and grateful as I put on my First Lady hat once again, loved on the members, and grew in my Christian walk.

I AM A VICTOR!

This opportunity, however, would be short-lived. About 18 months into pastoring the church, I felt like someone hit the rewind button, which sent me back in time. After a Sunday morning worship service, a meeting was held between my husband and church leaders. I sat quietly and prayed fervently as I observed my husband repeatedly attempt to defend his faithfulness to God, his love of pastoring, and his commitment to the church. Unfortunately, the leaders disagreed, and the outcome resulted in irreconcilable differences. Blind-sided by this untimely situation and not wanting to divide the church, we prayed and ultimately decided to leave. Once more, I dealt with my heart being broken, relationships being severed, and my faith being tested. This time I was at a familiar crossroad in my life, but I still wondered if I would get another opportunity to serve as the First Lady and come to love another congregation. Would I overcome this round of church hurt and walk alongside my husband while being tested in the fire, yet again?

As I think about how all of these tests and trials that caused me pain and anguish could have taken me out, I can't help but wonder how many women are walking in my shoes—feeling rejected, confused, and embarrassed about where their journey has taken them. How many women are suffering in silence in the pews, feeling betrayed by others, and wearing a mask to disguise their distress? How many women are yearning for other women to reciprocate their desire to belong in a genuine relationship? How many women are moved to take their husband by the hand and say, yes, I'll go through the fire with you?

After the second bout of church conflict occurred, it was then that the turning point came in my life when I realized that I could only control what Pam says or does; not what others say or do. God was that unseen guest all along as I went through the fiery tests. I decided to forgive those who had hurt my family and me, which led me to release the bitterness that I had harbored in my heart. Can you say "FREEDOM"? I am now free to move forward and do the great and mighty works that God planned for my life. I am a victor over the church hurt that I felt for years. I praise God for revealing the empowerment of lifting my voice, which I had suppressed for so long. My trials birthed a passion in me to start my business where I encourage, equip, and empower clergy wives to embrace their authentic selves, amplify their voices, and build meaningful relationships within a community of unique women.

Life is a series of explorations and discoveries about self. While walking through the fiery challenges of life, I've had to search the depths of my heart to find the essence of who I am. I discovered that it all starts with my mindset. God was with me all the time, and I was blessed through the test! I now embrace my authentic self by looking at the woman in the mirror every day and confessing that I am God's beloved daughter. I amplify my voice by coaching clergy wives who seek to make a difference in the lives of others they serve in ministry. I also cultivate relationships within a community of my fellow Sisters as we bond through our commonalities as clergy wives.

My unwavering passion for these beautiful women of God has led me to create Uniquely You Sis, an organization for women struggling with loneliness, isolation, and despair, have a yearning to be in sincere relationships, and desire to show the world their authentic self as a clergy wife. The organization is grounded in Key V.A.L.U.E.S., which are essential for Unlocking Possibilities, Surpassing Probabilities & Seizing Opportunities in clergy marriage, ministry, and more.

6 Key V.A.L.U.E.S. for Clergy Wives

*V*alue your unique role

*A*lways put family first

*L*ead with passion

*U*se your influence

*E*mbrace your calling

*S*hare your experiences

I AM A VICTOR!

Three things for a Clergy Wife to consider in her unique role. Just be…

1. open-minded to new people, perspectives, and predicaments.
2. prepared for the unthinkable, unimaginable, and the uncontrollable.
3. your authentic self as you explore, discover, and love the woman in the mirror.

Cultivating relationships with loyal friends and trusted mentors, many who are clergy wives, is important to me, but God is my ultimate provider, protector, and friend. I sense there are numerous clergy wives who, like me, are being tried in the fire and desire to be blessed through the test. You have the desire to overcome life's challenges, but you're stuck, fearful, or unsure how to take the first step. You want others to appreciate your God-given gifts, hear your powerful voice, and feel your joyful spirit. God has divinely called and placed you on this amazing journey to lead, love, and laugh alongside your husband, just as you are. Maya Angelou said, "Every journey begins with a single step." So, come on, my Sister. Seek God's presence now as you take that first step today!

BIO
Clergy Wives Coach | Speaker | Minister

Dr. Pam Smith enthusiastically lives out her passion of coaching clergy wives. She is the founder of Uniquely You Sis, LLC, and host of Let's Chat S.I.S., (Sisters Inspiring Sisters), an online chat where clergy wives express themselves in a no-judgment zone.

She teaches the realities of clergy family life in her course—The Clergy Family: After the Benediction. Dr. Smith also facilitates candid conversations with clergy couples and clergywomen.

As president of Smith Bios Group, Inc., she conducts health and wellness workshops. She enjoys spending time with her husband, Antonio, two daughters, son-in-love, and three grandsons.

Dr. Smith holds a Bachelor's degree in Communication Studies from UNC Charlotte, a Master's degree in Strategic Leadership from Mountain State University, and a doctorate in the Integration of Religion and Society from Oxford Graduate School.

Website: http://www.uniquelyyousis.com
Email: drpam@uniquelyyousis.com
Instagram: @drpam22

I AM A VICTOR!

SABRINA THOMAS

INHALE CONFIDENCE & EXHALE DOUBT
BY SABRINA THOMAS

"Overcoming self-doubt doesn't happen overnight. If you keep trying every day, you'll eventually see that every tiny step you make towards conquering it makes a difference."
Sabrina Thomas

A few years shy of turning 50 years old, I decided to leave the safety net of a 'traditional' career of over 20 years in hospitality and leaped into entrepreneurship. But plagued by self-doubt and consumed by fear of the unknown, I delayed my progress for a short period of time. It was only when I found a professional community of women who helped me change my mindset and outlook that I set off on a path to success, one step at a time.

I have always been enthusiastic and compassionate, so I was a natural at pre-empting customers' needs in the hotel industry. Working with large groups, I thrived on the bustle and constant change. But watching powerful women in that environment who owned businesses, spoke in front of crowds, and authored multiple bestsellers planted a seed of hope in my mind that I could do and be more.

When I was not working in hospitality, which I did enjoy, I was at home with my two sons, one of whom has special needs. Through the years, I had spent many hours, days, and months advocating for his right to education, care, inclusion, and acceptance. This was when I realized I wanted to do more. I wanted to "Be the Change" and advocate for families with special needs. I began to wonder whether I could do what I was so passionate about and get paid to do it by becoming a speaker.

But fear and lack of confidence crept in, and for at least two more years, I did nothing more than 'wish' and talk myself out of opportunities. Not only was I scared of starting, but I was not confident in my abilities. The truth is: CONFIDENCE is built with time. I am not sure why, but at some point, I had begun to believe the opposite of what God said about me. I believed the voice in my head that success was for 'someone else,' someone who deserves it. Proverbs 4:23 (NCV) says, "Be careful what you think because your thoughts run your life." This was true for me.

Slowly I started attending conferences and training courses, and I even hired a business coach. I could not understand why I was so self-assured in other areas of my life, but I had such a lack of confidence when it came to entrepreneurship. The biggest change in me occurred when I started following women leaders who were doing something similar to what I wanted to do but who were fifty steps ahead of me. They were powerhouses, and to be honest, I never wanted to copy them or be exactly like them; I just wanted to be successful. I wanted to create my own path.

I connected to a circle of women entrepreneurs and potential entrepreneurs who changed my outlook completely. Together we encouraged each other, gave feedback, challenged, and uplifted one another. It was an uncomfortable process at first, but it's only when the mirror is held up in front of you that you truly see yourself. It took prayer, focus, determination, and accountability to identify and name my destructive thought patterns and negate them with the truth. My biggest obstacle was inside of me, and only I could decide to do something about it.

Once I started to change my mindset, everything changed. Opportunities seemed to come my way more often, or perhaps I just accepted them more often. And when I finally started co-authoring books, I later realized that writing was a form of speaking. I was still using my voice; it was just on a different platform.

I have since co-authored over ten books, became a columnist, a speaker, and grown within my advocacy as well. I use my God-given gifts, and I am growing every day.

> *"When you believe in yourself, you can overcome self-doubt and have the confidence to act and get things done."*

If you want to start your own business or just grow within your current career and you are struggling with self-doubt and fear, you are not alone. Some of the most successful business leaders in history struggled with a lack of confidence. Think about the many successful inventions birthed from what seemed like a failure. Just because you feel fear doesn't mean you have to act on it.

Set some easy-win goals. You need long-term goals, but you also need some short-term attainable goals. In the beginning, my goal was to co-author one book and get a speaking engagement. I started small however my goals are now much bigger. If you make mistakes (and you will make mistakes), give them to God and forgive yourself. Take the time to learn from it, so you don't make the same mistakes again, and then get up and move on.

Here are four quick tips to help you if you feel like you're standing at the edge of a successful life, but you are too overwhelmed to take the next step:

FIND A TRIBE
I can't stress this enough. Finding people who support you, cheer for you, and don't always agree with you, is a rare but powerful thing. The beauty of having a support system is that on days when you are feeling

down, someone else will be there to help you up, and vice versa. Keep the communication lines open and give as much as you receive in these forums. Hold each other accountable and keep it real. You serve no one by being anything less than the true version of yourself.

You can start by finding online or local groups specific to your goal. There are many support groups for aspiring authors, speakers, start-up founders, and coaches. Attend the networking events and give of your knowledge and time to build these important relationships.

STOP WORRYING ABOUT WHAT OTHERS THINK

You must stop worrying about what other people think and focus on building yourself and your confidence. It changes your perspective of yourself, and you get to know your strengths and weaknesses. You will slowly start to believe in yourself and what you can achieve.

Focus on your goals, big or small. Work towards achieving them, even if they seem scary or you are worried about what people might say. Own your goals. Decide for yourself what you want out of life.

There will always be people in your life who don't have your best interest at heart, and even those who love you but don't know what's best for you. Do what you need to do for your own mental, physical, and spiritual health.

DON'T COMPARE

Stop comparing yourself to people with different gifts, backgrounds, and life choices. You were made with unique talents, and your circumstances are your own. What you see online is seldom a true reflection of the sacrifices people you look up to have made to get where they are.

If I compared my success to that of women who don't have the same responsibilities as I do or who were years ahead of me, it would be a disservice to me. When we compare ourselves to other people and judge ourselves and our progress by that comparison, we are setting ourselves up for failure.

My hospitality background, personality, and empathy for others have uniquely equipped me for the work I do. Looking back, I realize that all the small steps I took daily added up to the results I see today. It didn't happen overnight.

PUSH YOURSELF

The presence of fear is not proof that you are making a mistake. A healthy amount of fear is natural when we are doing and learning new things. Challenge yourself to do things outside your comfort zone, like meeting with prospective clients or negotiating margins with suppliers. Only when you stretch yourself will you know what you can achieve. Celebrate the wins. I think you will be surprised at what you can achieve when you put your mind to it.

Today I can say I am a victor over self-doubt. It has taken me years, and I still have days where I struggle, but I have learned that by trusting God and taking one small step at a time, I can overcome any self-limiting beliefs that pop up.

You can achieve more than you think. Don't sell yourself short. You are equipped for the work only you can do. My life is proof that self-doubt doesn't have to be a life sentence.

"There are always obstacles on the way to success, but no obstacle is big enough that you can't overcome. The biggest one, though, is your own limiting belief and self-doubt. If you can find the confidence and belief in yourself, there is nothing else you can't overcome.

BIO

Sabrina Thomas is an Author, Parent Coach, Speaker, Columnist, and passionate Autism & Special Education Advocate who empowers parents to become their child's best advocate.

Sabrina is a mother of two beautiful sons, one of whom has special needs. She has a drive sparked and fueled by her experience as a mother of a special need's son. She works with the vision of educating, empowering, and supporting special needs families through her advocacy.

Sabrina's compassion combined with her love for her son and appreciation for all people living with special needs are the driving force behind her awareness initiatives.

With over 19 years of experience as an advocate she has become a strong voice in her field. Sabrina's mission is to serve as a voice for the specials needs community and ensure families never go at it alone and always feel supported.

Website: www.sabrinatspeaks.com
Facebook: @sabrinatspeaks
Instagram: @sabrinatspeaks

I AM A VICTOR!

STEPHANIE WALL

SORRY MA: A STORY OF BLENDED STORIES IN MAMA'S TEARS
BY STEPHANIE WALL

It was happening again; Ma was looking at me for what seemed like a very long time. What is that look that I see in her eyes? Streams of tears are rolling down her face. It's not anger or fear. I cannot put my finger on it; suddenly, it dawns on me. My chest feels tight like someone is sitting on it. The room feels smaller than it is. I notice hot tears rolling down my cheeks and into my mouth. I keep wiping my eyes with the back of my hand because I can't see and am trying to be sure of what I am seeing in Ma's eyes. My inner voice screams it's "PITY" mixed with heartbreak and shame coming from my mother's eyes. She looks like a wounded puppy. Or is it the look she had at that last funeral? I had seen it before. However, today, it is stinging.

There was that time when I was 14, and I missed my period, and she had to take me to see her doctor, which at the time she called "the doctor that checked female parts." It was a very uncomfortable visit. The doctor was a tall white guy with white and black hair and a beard. After taking off all my clothes and putting on a gown, a lady nurse and my mom were in the room as he did a check of my "lady parts." I held my eyes closed tight. I had never experienced anything like this. I was so embarrassed. After the exam was complete, he told my mother that I was pregnant. She burst into tears and began to wail. There were no questions asked about how it happened. A few days later, I was whisked off to a clinic where a procedure to terminate the pregnancy was performed. It was awful, painful, and humiliating. I cried for a week, and my soul cried for a lifetime.

There were a few other times, including when we were told that I was expelled from school. Oh, and the time she cried at the wedding between a man, who physically beat me, causing black eyes, and me. I am sorry, Ma. You see, we only meet our parents when we are born. For many reasons, my mom's generation did not talk about past hurts. So generational trauma continued to get passed down. I did not learn about Ma's past traumas until I was in my mid 20's. By then, I had experienced a great deal of trauma. Why didn't I know that Ma had given birth to our brother at age 14? There are a lot of rumors about how she came to be pregnant. As a result of this pregnancy, she never finished high school, thus never obtained a high school diploma. She later married our dad, which ended with a broken heart after over ten years of marriage and four kids. She later married again for the wrong reasons. Are you starting to get a clear picture of why Ma cried? She saw herself in that doctor's office. She saw herself in that office at the school; she knew I was getting married for all the wrong reasons. Just as she did, with her second husband. Ma just did not or could not find the words to tell me so.

I have heard various analogies about butterflies. The one that sticks with me is this. "Everyone wants to be a butterfly; its beauty is well known. However, before the butterfly becomes a butterfly, it is first a caterpillar that has to go through a transformation." In his book "Crushing," Bishop T.D. Jakes talks about having to go through the dirty places. He even talks about his daughter having a baby at age 14. I could have used a dose of truth back in the day that is now readily available in books. Like most kids of my generation, I had a Sunday school spiritual foundation. This foundation set the stage for a parallel existence. I did not know it, but God would show me that He was with me the whole time. While growing through my storm as an adult, a co-worker invited me to his family bible study; from there, I began to lean on my faith and use God's word in rebuke of all that was going on in my life.

I AM A VICTOR!

It seemed like overnight. I went from a self-described disappointment to one victory after the other. Like Paris Hilton, D.L Hughley, Nicolas Cage, Jay-Z, Peter Jennings, Quentin Tarintino, Elton Jon, Beyonce, and many others, I obtained my high school equivalency (G.E.D). It would have been easier to graduate with my peers than trying to obtain that G.E.D. I had to know a little about some subjects that I had never taken, nor would I have been required to take to graduate with my peers. My life began to evolve quickly; doors were closing and opening like crazy. Yes, I was still in the storm; but I was getting stronger. I AM A VICTOR! I stopped believing what others said about me and started believing what God said about ME. In a matter of months and years, I learned to love myself, took course after course on personal development, got away from destructive people and behaviors, remarried, completed college earning two degrees, including a master's degree, gave birth to two sons, was blessed with a bonus son and now three granddaughters. I retired from a career after 20 years of service, where I was able to serve and protect those who are often invisible/under-served/dismissed.

I AM A VICTOR! I am often asked what advice I have for people who may be living through similar situations. There is no one size fits all. I can only tell you what helped me and what has helped my clients and many others I have encountered over the years. First, believe in something bigger than yourself and the human race. The Bible verse that sustains me is: "I can do all things through Christ, who strengths me" (Philippians 4:13). Second, seek professional help. There is no shame in talking to a professional to process life. If you do not deal with it, it will show up in other negative ways in your life. You will bleed on folks that had nothing to do with the pain. According to the American Psychological Association: Traumatic events can result in serious stress and detrimental consequences for survivors who are women and their families. Approximately one half (50 percent) of all individuals will be exposed to at least one traumatic event in their lifetime. Although many individuals will absorb the trauma over time, many survivors will experience long-lasting problems.

Have real conversations with your children about polarizing experiences that you have had to reduce passing on trauma. You will fall down, but as artist & songwriter Donny McClurkin says, "You can get back up again." Below are a few of the resources that are available today that may or may not have been available when I was growing through it. Do NOT count yourself out. Do NOT let anyone else count you out.

- Crisis Text Line | Text HOME To 741741 free, 24/7 Crisis Counseling
- Domestic Violence Support | The National Domestic Violence Hotline (thehotline.org)
- Inspiring List of 50 Successful People Who Have A GED (bestgedclasses.org)
- Financial Aid for Moms | Landing Pages (educationconnection.com)
- Books that changed my life:
  - Battlefield-Mind-Spiritual-Growth-Winning_ ~ Joyce Meyers
  - Women's Bible NIV o I know why the caged bird sings ~ Maya Angelou
  - The Lady, Her Love & Her Lord ~ Bishop T.D. Jakes
  - Woman Thou Art Loosed ~ Bishop T.D. Jakes
- Physical things that changed my life:
  - I began to exercise
  - I changed my hairstyle/color
  - I began to dress like the successful women in my head
  - I began to visit more museums
  - I spent more time with my kids outdoors
  - I took classes at the local community college
  - I created vision boards
- Mental Habits I formed:
  - I prayed and often meditated
  - I recited positive affirmations
  - I changed my circle o   I read self-help books
  - I served others

I AM A VICTOR!

I have a lot of people to thank for my success, including "Ma," who before her death, on Thanksgiving 2007, did still cry. However, I saw tears of joy run down her face; when I remarried, completed college courses, moved into our new home, and as she watched me mature as a woman of faith, as a leader in the community. I learned that "Ma" might not have known a lot, but she knew how to pray. I am sorry, Ma. I now know that there were blended stories in your TEARS. You cried because you loved me! I love and miss you, Ma! I AM A VICTOR!

BIO
Entrepreneur | Speaker | Author | Certified Coach

She is affectionately known as "TOP" (Tower of Power) due to her infectious energy that draws people to her and fills a room. She has a passion for helping women to break barriers to self-esteem. As an author & survivor of domestic abuse, Stephanie understands life's struggles. She shares her story to empower others through her life's story in a book titled How My Part-time Job Saved My Life: A True Story of Overcoming Abuse and Claiming a Victorious Life and as a contributing author in other books.

Stephanie has a master's degree from Johns Hopkins University in Management & Organizational Leadership. She is a proud wife, a loving mother of three adult sons, three beautiful granddaughters, and a daughter-in-love.

Her favorite quote is

"Life's most persistent and urgent question is, what are you doing for others"?
Dr. Martin Luther King Jr.

https://speakerstephanie.com